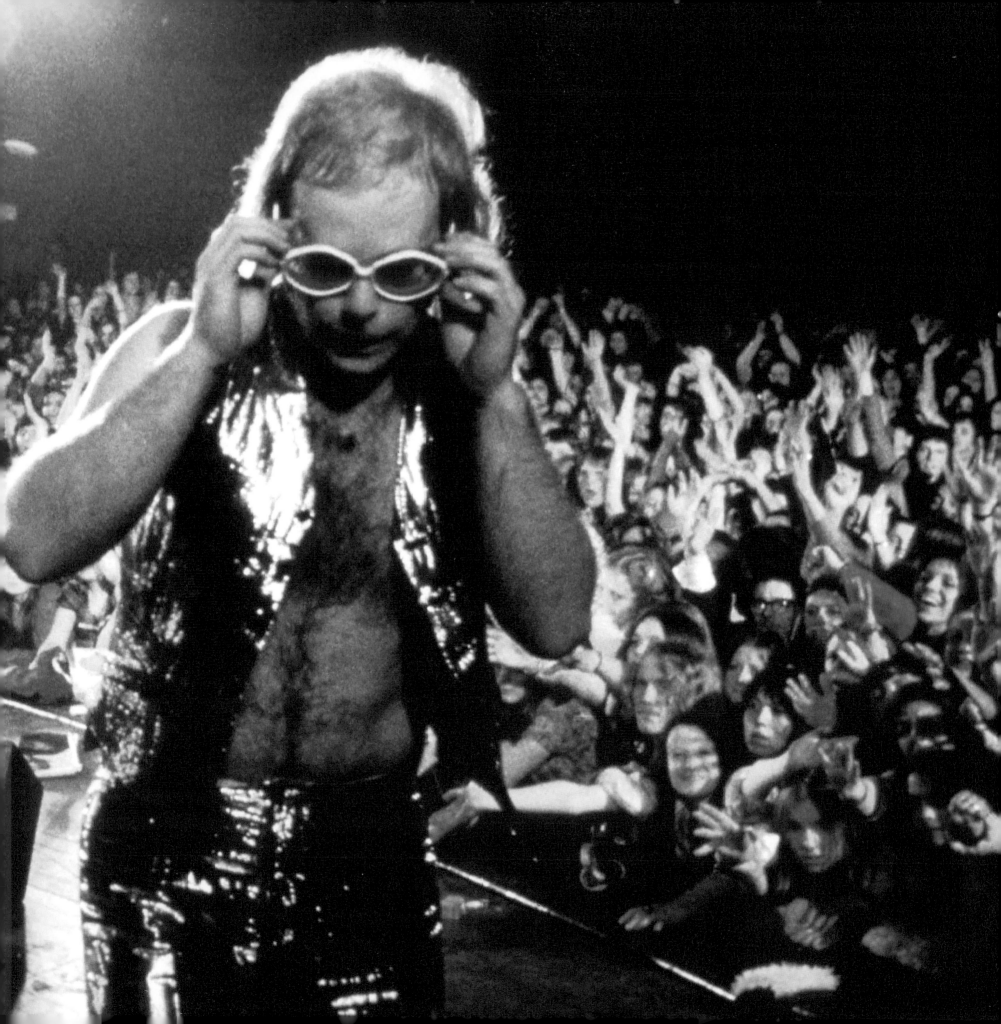

ELTON JOHN

JOHN

THIS ONE'S FOR YOU

A Life in Music

Danann
BOOKS

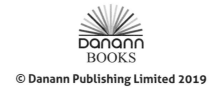

CONTENTS

INTRODUCTION

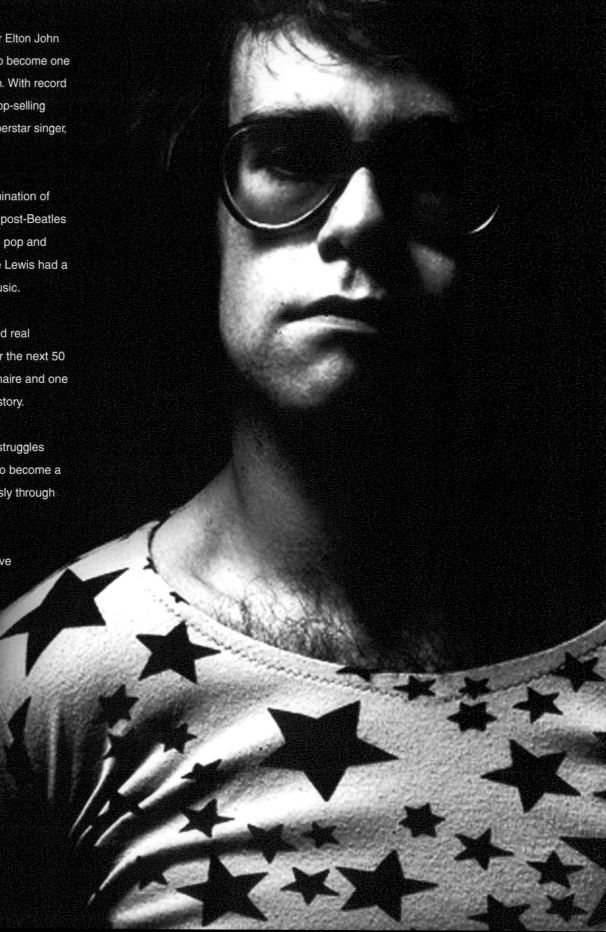

During a dazzling 50-year musical career, Sir Elton John has risen from playing the piano in a pub to become one of the biggest musical stars in a generation. With record sales of over 300 million, he is one of the top-selling solo artists of all time — a multi-award-winning global superstar singer, songwriter and performer.

His 1970 breakthrough single Your Song began his domination of the pop charts and established his credentials to fill the post-Beatles landscape with his unique take on piano-based ballads, pop and rock. Not since 1950s stars Little Richard and Jerry Lee Lewis had a man and his piano made such an impact on modern music.

Few would have imagined that Elton's early success and real emotional connection with fans would be sustained over the next 50 years to see him become a singer-songwriter extraordinaire and one of the most successful musical theatre composers in history.

Flamboyant and prone to excess, Elton has overcome struggles with drink, drugs, food and his sexuality along the way to become a notable fundraiser and charity campaigner, most famously through the Elton John AIDS Foundation.

Now happily married with two sons, Elton's priorities have changed and he has announced his retirement from performing after 2021.

This is his story ● ● ● ● ● ● ● ● ● ●

WHEN ROCK WAS YOUNG

1947 - 61

When Sir Elton John was born as Reginald Kenneth Dwight on March 25, 1947 in a council house in a dreary post-war London suburb, the odds that he would become a rich, famous and flamboyant rock star were pretty long.

The first, and as it turned out the only, child of unremarkable parents Sheila and Stanley Dwight of Pinner, little Reggie, as he was called, entered a world where life was rather grim.

The UK was just emerging from one of the hardest winters on record, including freezing temperatures, gale force winds and a succession of heavy snowstorms. Still recovering from the effects of the Second World War, the country was riven with difficulties including shortages of food and coal — rationing was still the norm.

So the wealth and worldwide success little Reggie would come to enjoy as Elton John would have been unimaginable to his parents. They wouldn't even have been able to define the term *'global superstar'* as there was no such thing at the time.

Elton's parents had met during the war in 1942 when his father Stan was 17 and in the RAF and Sheila was 16 and working in an office. They married in 1945 and — as was common among young couples at that time — set up home with Sheila's family, comprising parents Ivy and Fred, sister Win and brother Reginald, young Reggie's namesake.

After the war ended, Stan stayed on in the RAF and subsequently was often posted away so that Reggie spent most of his formative years in the company of Sheila, nan Ivy and aunt Win, who became major influences in his life.

Stan was posted to Basra, Iraq in 1949 and rather than go with him, Sheila decided that she and Reggie, not yet two years old, would do better to stay with her family. A few years later Stan's posting to Wiltshire as a squadron leader provided the family with another opportunity to live together. Although Sheila gave it a go, she didn't appear to enjoy the life of an officer's wife and before long she left Stan to it and returned home, with Reggie, to her family in Pinner.

While Sheila and Stan were evidently having problems in their marriage, Reggie's early childhood was apparently quite happy as he was indulged and protected by the coterie of his admiring mother, grandmother and aunt. Speaking in 1995, Elton said that they were the people that he could *'really rely on for support and love.'* Nan Ivy looked after him while the others were working and is said to have given him his first go on the family piano.

Upright pianos were common in the most ordinary of households in the late 1940s and early 1950s — pre-television, when other entertainment was thin on the ground. Pianists were popular entertainers at that time — Trinidadian Winifred Atwell, who had a series of boogie-woogie, ragtime hits, was a major influence on young Reggie. Russ Conway was another favourite in the Dwight household, along with the flamboyant American Liberace, who was as famous in his time for his amazing outfits and joie de vivre at the piano as Reggie would come to be.

It was Nan Ivy who first sat Reggie at the piano when he was just three-years-old. He showed immediate natural aptitude and within a year was astounding his mother by picking out the classical standard, The Skaters' Waltz all by himself.

His innate and prodigious talent for picking up and playing music by ear was immediately apparent and so he was sent for proper piano lessons from the age of six. Reggie was always happy to perform and regularly

provided the entertainment at family parties, and later at school.

Aged 11 he won a place at the Royal Academy of Music on a part time junior scholarship scheme which had been set up to give opportunities to state school pupils. Saturday mornings would see him heading into central London for piano lessons at the Academy with his teacher Helen Piena who taught him a classical repertoire, alongside theory and composition.

Elton has since said that he didn't really enjoy classical music and could never have succeeded at it because his hands are *'too small and can barely cover an octave …these chipolata fingers are better for rock and roll'*.

But he dutifully continued his lessons and evidently has fond enough memories of the place because he has since established the Elton John Scholarship Fund which offers grants for budding talents to study at the Academy every year. He also accepted an honorary doctorate in 2002.

Despite his evident musical abilities, he didn't shine as brightly at school — satisfactory plodder would seem to sum up his school days. His appearance was also distinctly average — short, round-faced and wearing glasses he didn't have the look of a budding rock star.

But that's not to say that Reggie didn't have his passions – they just didn't lie in the classroom.

During his early teens he became a big fan of more hardcore rock and rollers including Little Richard and Jerry Lee Lewis who had a massive influence on him.

His parents collected records and a 26-year-old Elton later told Paul Gambaccini for Rolling Stone magazine that his musical career really began when he was old enough to start listening to them. *'The first records I ever heard were [late 1940 and 1950s stars] Kay Starr.. Billy May … Tennessee Ernie Ford….Les Paul and Mary Ford and Guy Mitchell. I grew up in that era.*

'I was three or four when I started listening to records like that. I obviously took great interest in them and then I went through the skiffle thing with Lonnie Donegan. The first records my mum brought home that I was really knocked out by were Hound Dog and Haley's ABC Boogie'.

As soon as he was old enough Reggie began a record collection of his own — his early purchases including At The Hop by Danny and the Juniors and Reet Petite by Jackie Wilson. His collection became vast; the precious discs were thoughtfully collected, carefully kept and meticulously catalogued. Alongside the records, his bedroom was full of other collections — Dinky Toys and Matchbox cars, sheet music and comics. Football — and Watford FC in particular — was another huge interest. Taken to matches by his father, Reggie first watched the team, nicknamed the *'Hornets'*, as a six-year-old, and the club was famously to become a lifelong love. Match programmes joined the other treasures in his bedroom.

His love for order and cataloguing, which continues today, had begun at this tender age, and whether young Reggie disappeared into his own world to seek solace from the disturbances in his family only he could know for sure. But certainly around this time the façade of Stan and Sheila's marriage came to an end. Their separations and rows had become more frequent and when Stan was posted to Harrogate in Yorkshire in 1960 he left for good — there really being no question of Sheila and Reggie going with him. They had been divorced in all but name for years — now it was time to make it official.

But in those days divorce was only possible on certain prescribed grounds. During Stan's periods working away Sheila had struck up a relationship with local builder and decorator Fred Farebrother and he was cited in the divorce which was granted on grounds of Sheila's adultery becoming absolute in 1962.

Elton's relationship with his father was evidently already fractured by their frequent separations and eventually it broke down altogether. He has since spoken of finding his father an intimidating presence. But, immediately following the divorce, the pair kept in touch for a while and Reggie seemed happy enough when his father remarried a few years later and produced another four sons.

But in years to come their relationship deteriorated further. In many interviews Elton describes his father in terms that are less than flattering. Evidently having looked back at their relationship over time he found his father to be wanting.

Perhaps it was that when Stan was around he would try to impose some greater discipline, or simply that his generation of men, who had served during the war, were less outwardly affectionate and emotional in their behaviour. But something went badly wrong in the relationship between father and son that was never mended; to the extent that they were not in touch for most of Reggie's adult life and — as Elton — he did not attend his father's funeral in 1991.

His fall out with his father was an early example of Reggie's (then Elton's) continuing need for those around him in any capacity to demonstrate total loyalty. He had no time for anyone who he felt had let him down.

The difficulties seem all the sadder because it appears to be from Stan that Reggie inherited his musical talent. Stan was a very competent trumpet player, while his own father, Reggie's grandfather Edwin, was a soprano cornet player. Yet Stan never once came to see his son shine on stage as a simply dazzling star performer.

I'M ÖNLY THE PIANO PLAYER

1962 - 69

While Stan's genes may well have bestowed the musical gifts and ability, it was Sheila and her family who provided the encouragement. She seemed less concerned than Stan when her new beau (and later husband) Fred, who grew close to Reggie, sorted him out with a job playing piano at a pub in Pinner, The Northwood Hills Hotel.

It wasn't a great venue but the work provided Reggie with performance opportunities and a few pounds in his pocket. Reggie had a regular weekend gig there for some two years. He was always happy to perform — his first adoring audience of Sheila, Ivy and Win had doubtless given him some confidence — and the odd drunk or punch-up never seemed to phase him. He wasn't at all precious about what he played — pounding out bar standards and taking requests with ease.

Although Stan was continuing to support Reggie financially, the earnings from the pub — supplemented by a nightly collection in a beer glass — came in very handy and allowed the purchase of an electric piano and amplifier, among other treats.

And of course most importantly the work got Reggie noticed. Before long he was invited to join a band called the Corvettes who gigged in church halls and youth clubs. This band morphed into Bluesology, a four-man rhythm and blues outfit with guitarists Stu Brown and Rex Bishop and drummer Mick Inkpen.

Doubtless emboldened by this opportunity, 17-year-old Reggie decided to throw his lot into music completely and quit school just a few months before he was due to take his A levels.

Stan was neither consulted nor happy about this decision. Reggie knew that his father did not consider a career in music

to be sensible. *'Dad wanted me to be something else …more respectable'*, Elton has said since.

This seems to have been a pivotal moment for Stan, who then appeared to accept that Fred Farebrother had replaced him in Reggie's life and affections.

Reggie was fond of Fred who he had nicknamed Derf (Fred backwards) and, although Fred didn't actually marry Sheila until 1972, did seem to view him as a father figure. Stan had remarried shortly after his divorce in 1962 but had remained in Essex, in part so that he was still close to Reg. But at this point, seemingly aware that his opinions carried no weight with Reg whatsoever, he left the south to go and live near his second wife Edna's original home in Cheshire.

But neither Stan's disapproval, nor the advice from his school and music teachers to go to university, dissuaded Reggie from his intended course of action.

However unlikely it might have seemed, he was determined to be a rock star and managed to get a job which took him a little nearer to that goal.

He found work as an office boy slap bang in the middle of London's music industry, at song publishers Mills Music.

Reggie had a cousin Roy Dwight, who was a professional footballer playing for Fulham and Nottingham Forest throughout the 1950s. As well as fuelling Reggie's love for football, Roy's success and relative fame at the time had another perk — some useful showbiz contacts. So he was able to wangle Reggie an introduction to Mills Music.

'Artistes, composers, singers, musicians, to form a *new group'*.

The company's offices were in Denmark Street, London, at the centre of the British music industry and home to most of the major music publishers and management companies of the day. It was certainly an ideal place for an aspiring rock star to work. Reggie was able to soak up the atmosphere as recording studios sprang up around the area and musicians lounged and networked in the coffee shops — famously La Gioconda.

By day Reggie worked on fairly menial tasks such as packing parcels and by night he was gigging with Bluesology. In 1965 the band had gained enough confidence and work to turn professional. They recorded a demo and were signed by Fontana Records. Their first two singles were both written by Reg, the main talent in the band, but neither his 1965 contribution Come Back Baby nor Mr Frantic the following year were successful.

However the band lived to fight another day. On their return from a tour of Germany, Reggie and the rest of the band were offered work backing visiting musicians from America. The first of these was the R&B singer Major Lance who, being one of Reggie's early idols, made a big impression on him. *'Backing Major Lance was probably the biggest thing that ever happened to me'*, Elton said years later.

Success with Major Lance led to more frequent and impressive bookings and Bluesology went on to back many renowned artists, including The Isley Brothers, Patti LaBelle and The Inkspots. Things were going so well that Reggie gave up his day job and by 1966 — with Bluesology expanding to become one of the top session bands in London — it seemed like the right decision.

But after a while, the gloss wore off these gigs. The work was hard, involving a punishing travel schedule, and the pay wasn't great. Brushes with fame, pounding the piano in the background, wasn't enough for an ambitious Reggie who wanted so much more.

He was feeling unfulfilled and marginalised in the band, not getting many opportunities to sing and frustrated at Bluesology's lack of success in its own right.

His time working in London had begun to change him. Mills Music offices had been close to Carnaby Street, centre of the fashion world, and having left his school uniform and warehouse overalls behind him, he had acquired a nascent interest in clothes.

But this passion for fashion was rather thwarted by his weight. Already of stocky build and with a round face — both the result of genes from Stan again — his looks began to suffer from the unhealthy life on the road which caused him to put on weight. He was also experiencing his first problems with his hair — having always been thin it was now also receding which was a very unwelcome development for a 19-year-old wannabe rock star.

Then something happened to shake life up a bit. In 1966 the popular R&B guitarist and singer Long John Baldry invited Bluesology to become his regular band.

Baldry — named Long John because he was 6ft 7ins tall — was a commanding figure in other ways too. He was an affable, foppish-looking character, fond of good clothes, with a wonderfully rich, Deep Southern sounding voice which was rather at odds with his dandyish appearance.

The members of Bluesology — now in yet another and expanded line up — were similarly kitted out in suits and frilly shirts. But the outfits and the step up the musical hierarchy still wasn't enough for Reg who was by now wholly disenchanted. Where he had previously been a funny and engaging personality, a great mimic who was entertaining company, he had now become less chirpy and inclined to disappear into the dressing room in a mood — an early manifestation of what were to become know as *'Elton's little moments'*. The diet pills he was popping weren't helping either.

With Long John Baldry on vocals and other band members chosen to provide back up ahead of him, Reggie was sidelined. The music was becoming more cabaret-style following Baldry's 1967 hit Let The Heartaches Begin and Reg had had enough.

Looking for a new direction, his prayers were answered when he spotted an advert from Liberty Records — one of his favourite American labels which was looking to set up a European division. *'Liberty wants talent'* the advert read. *'Artistes, composers, singers, musicians, to form a new group'*. Reg duly presented himself at their London offices.

His audition wasn't amazing but he did enough to warrant the chance to make a demo. During his time in the recording studio he mentioned to the head of A&R Ray Williams that while composition was his forte, he didn't really have a flair for lyrics. Instead of kicking him out the door, which must have been an option, Ray remembered another letter he'd received in response to the advert. It was from a young lyricist called Bernie Taupin. He handed Reg a sheaf of poems from Bernie and told him to see what he could do with them.

It was kismet.

• • • • ──────────────────────────▶
One of Elton John First publicity pictures in Hampstead

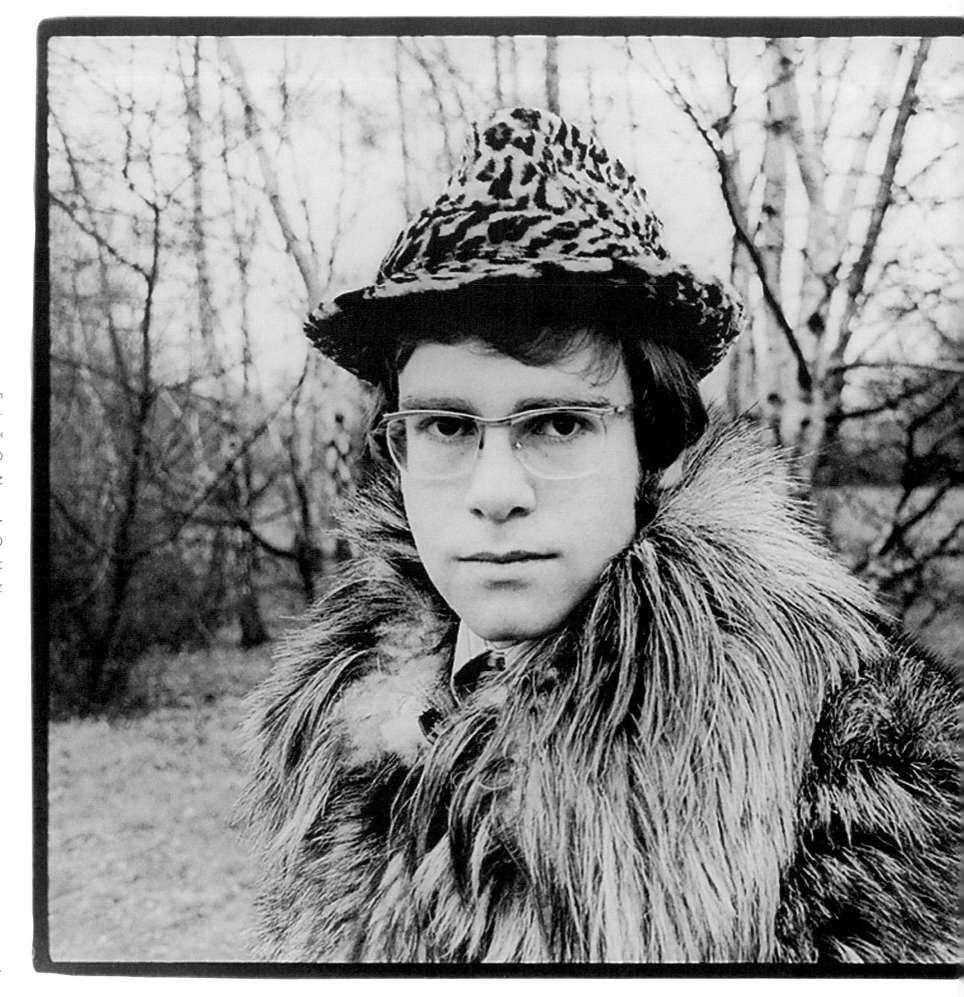

In the end nothing came of the opportunity with Liberty as although Ray Williams was certain Reg had talent, he couldn't convince his bosses of the fact. But the meeting had been pivotal as, going out on a limb, Ray introduced Reg to music publisher Dick James, who had worked with the Beatles.

As Ray's protégé piano player, Reg now got the chance to work for Dick's company Dick James Music (DJM) writing songs for all the company's contracted performers. Ray was also good to his word and set up a meeting with Bernie Taupin. Reg had liked Bernie's lyrics, feeling an immediate connection and finding that they suggested melodies to him.

At their eventual meeting Bernie and Reg liked one another on sight. Although Bernie was three years younger and from a happy family in the Lincolnshire countryside, as opposed to Reggie's less happy big city background, the young men had much in common and felt comfortable in each other's company. They shared a shy demeanour and a feeling of being different, but also a strong sense of what they wanted to do.

They quickly found they had shared interests, especially in music and song writing, and decided to work together. They became firm friends, establishing a brotherly relationship which has lasted ever since. The formation of Elton and Bernie, as a brilliant songwriting partnership as strong and successful as any that had gone before them, had begun.

While Reg was still frequently on the road with Bluesology, Bernie would post his esoteric *'Procol Harum- ish'* lyrics to Reg who would then compose the music. The method of working suited both men and continued long after it was strictly necessary.

One of Elton John First publicity pictures in Hampstead

In November 1967 Bernie and Reg signed a contract with DJM and Reg took a leap of faith and left the band left Bluesology a month later.

But before he left, there was one final matter to attend to — Reg had long understood that his name was hardly the stuff of rock and roll dreams. He decided to embark on the new phase of his career with DJM with a new name and didn't need to look far.

He simply took the Christian name of his band mate, saxophonist Elton Dean and combined it with Baldry's Christian name. Elton John was born.

For the next couple of years, Elton wrote songs for DJM with Bernie, and supplemented his income by working as a session pianist and back up vocalist. His *'apprenticeship'* with Bluesology had prepared him well for life as a jobbing musician and he was always happy to work hard and pick up sessions as a pianist and vocalist. His talent for mimicry came in handy as he covered popular songs for anonymous cover version albums. These budget-priced collections of sound-alike current hit singles were very popular at the time. But although they were a source of cash, the work was a million miles from what Elton had in mind for himself.

But at last things really started to happen for him when a new producer, Steve Brown joined DJM with a brief to nurture the Elton/Bernie partnership. He gave them inspiration and a new creative direction and their songwriter improved.

In January 1969 Elton and Bernie got a song released for themselves, *'Lady Samantha'*. The song wasn't a commercial hit but received critical acclaim and a lot of radio play. Its success in being accepted for the Radio 1 playlist and getting a mention by John

Peel, meant the duo were looked at with new respect and offered a chance to record an album.

They also reached the final stage of the UK's televised search for a Eurovision song in 1969. Lulu had been chosen to perform the UK's entry in the Eurovision Song Contest — a massive deal in those days — and sang each of six possible entries from which BBC viewers would choose the UK's entry on her Saturday night television show's *'A Song for Europe'* segment. Song number four was I Can't Go On Living Without You written by Elton and Bernie. But it failed to impress the voters coming last with 5,087 votes, as opposed to the 56,476 cast for the winning entry Boom Bang -a- Bang.

Undeterred, the songwriting partners carried on. By that time they were living together with Sheila and Fred. As Bernie knew no one in London it was decided that to further their working partnership it made sense for him to move to London and live with Reg and his mother and stepfather at their home in Frome Court. Elton has described Bernie as being *'like a brother …we were inseparable'*.

When Elton left home to move in with his first girlfriend, Bernie came too and lived in the spare room.

The girlfriend was Linda Ann Woodrow, an unlikely first love with her being three years his senior, as tall as Elton was short, as independent as Elton was mollycoddled and — as heir to the Epicure pickles company — as rich as Elton was poor.

They got as far as getting engaged on Elton's 21st birthday and wedding plans were underway — but then Elton evidently decided he couldn't go through with it. In what seemed to be more of a gesture than a wholehearted suicide attempt, he stuck his head

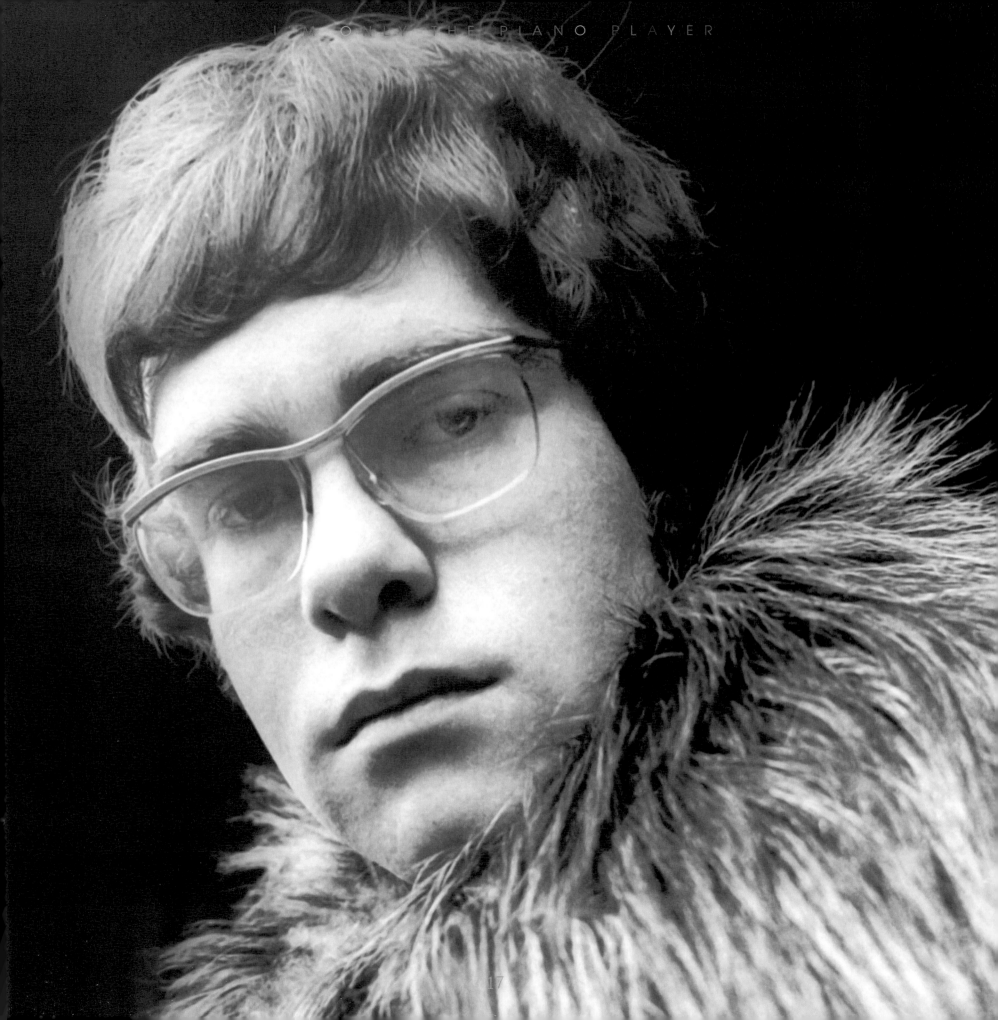

in the oven at their flat … Bernie rescued him and the pair moved back to Sheila and Fred's in Pinner.

While returning home might have seemed a backward step, in fact it was a good move. Their song writing went from strength to strength and the pair were happy and productive as Sheila looked after them both.

So they had plenty of time to concentrate on producing an eclectic collection of songs for, Empty Sky — Elton's first and often over-looked album, which was released in June 1969.

With Elton on vocals and piano, the album featured several musicians who would go on to work with Elton over the years; including Caleb Quaye on guitars and conga drums Tony Murray on bass guitar, Roger Pope on drums, Don Fay on tenor sax and flute, and Graham Vickery on harmonica. Nigel Olsen, who went on to work with Elton for years to come, also featured on one track, Lady What's Tomorrow.

By today's standards **the album** sounds rather rough **around** the edges, **but Elton's** talent is clearly heard.

Surprisingly, the opening track and title song on this very first album opens not with piano, but with a full minute of conga drums, before a piano-driven bluesy sound takes over. Very much redolent of its time, the whole recording has hints of the psychedelia which

was so popular in the late 1960s. While it doesn't include any standout hits, it shows Elton's potential. The best-known track from the album is Skyline Pigeon which retained some life after the album and is still sometimes played live today.

DJM mounted a massive publicity drive to support the album, including a rather enigmatic poster campaign on the back of London buses. While this created a bit of a buzz around Elton, actual album sales were disappointing at around 4,000 copies — a blow to Elton who craved chart success.

Fortunately for him, commercial success was not the be all and end all for a talented musician at that time. British record companies still offered a period of artist growth and development and did not look for a financial return from the start. So they didn't routinely get rid of people who failed to achieve success with a first album.

But even Elton was pushing his luck. By now DJM had spent the equivalent today of around half a million pounds on developing and promoting him. However, Steve Brown persuaded the powers above that Elton be allowed to build on the progress made on Empty Sky. He generously fell on his sword and said that he believed a new producer was needed.

So a second album was **given the green light and Elton – and Bernie – lived to fight another day.**

Elton John poses for a portrait with his lyricist Bernie Taupin in 1969, London

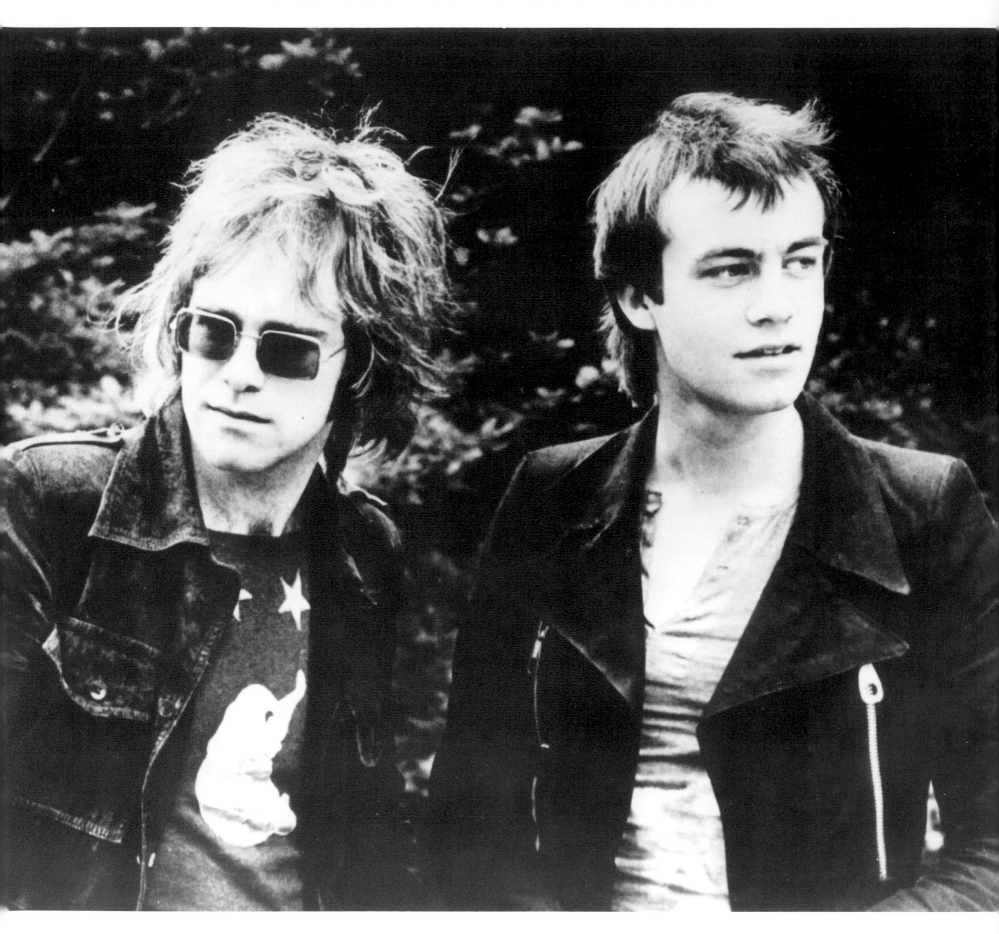

ROCKET MAN TAKES OFF

More luck came in the form of two experienced record makers persuaded to work with a then unknown Elton.

Producer Gus Dudgeon and arranger Paul Buckmaster were hot tickets, fresh from their phenomenal success working on Space Oddity for David Bowie. That record was revolutionary. Both men were impressed enough by Elton's work to take on production of his crucial second album.

Elton was almost overwhelmed by the effort and talent being brought to bear on what was effectively his last chance — the self-titled album Elton John. But his classical training paid off as Paul Buckmaster brought in a full symphony orchestra and Elton was able to step up to the mark. *'I was scared stiff having to play live with the orchestra, but it gave me backbone, resolve and experience',* Elton says of the recording.

Once again the tracks were a real mix of styles, poetic lyrics crafted by Bernie and haunting chords from Elton. But the big differences this time were a more complex, richly layered recording and a virtuoso vocal — Elton was singing his heart out in his last chance saloon. Now 23 his voice had matured and was less *'reedy'* and more controlled.

The opening track is the seminal *'Your Song'.* Urged to write from the heart Bernie had disregarded the fact that as a teenager he had little experience of romantic love, and simply imagined that he had a girl friend and wrote the simple and innocent, almost conversational lyrics with universal, cross-generational appeal.

Speaking in 2916 Elton recalled, *'When I wrote that in 1970 …. Bernie came to me with the lyric and I read it through and thought this is amazing for an 18-year-old boy to write this lyric. When I finished*

playing it for him I think we both realised that this was a huge step forward in our songwriting. We never looked back from that song.'

Writing on his website in 2018 Bernie said; I thought it might be timely to correct the massive amount of misinformation regarding how the lyrics to "Your Song" were originally conceived. Normally, things of this nature and the rewriting of history in order to entertain and enable people's preferred fantasies are of little or no concern to me. However, in the case of this popular composition, the story behind how I came to write the lyrics is such a bloated and widespread fairy tale that it's time the set the record straight.

'It's everywhere, unfortunately. Google it and the truth is hard to find. Wikipedia have it wrong, assorted fan pages and songwriting sites buy into the myth, and sadly, even Universal Music Group, which administers our catalog, carries the big fib on its online website!

'I can only assume that the invention is more appealing than the actual truth. The truth being that I scribbled the lyric down on a lined notepad at the kitchen table of Elton's mother's apartment in the London suburb of Northwood Hills, breakfast time sometime in 1969. That's it. Plain and simple. It was not to my recollection inspired by anyone, although at the time Elton secretly thought it was. However, that element will have to remain a grey area along with what perpetrated the widely circulated alternate version of the true story, and where and when it first appeared.

'So, supposedly I wrote the lyrics on the roof of 20 Denmark Street in London's Tin Pan Alley while waiting for Elton to finish work, hence, "I sat on the roof and kicked off the moss."

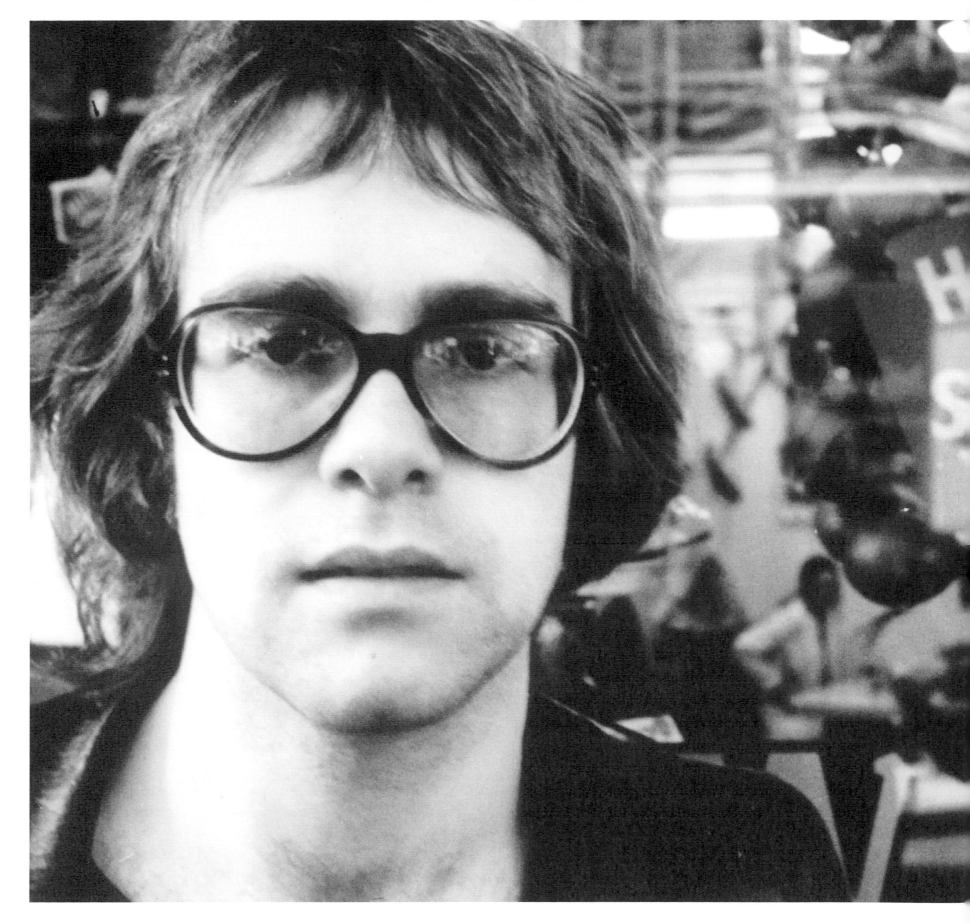

↑ Elton John poses for a portrait with his band members
Dee Murray (left) and Nigel Olsson, 1970

← • • • •

Elton John poses for a portrait wearing glasses in front of
a sign that says 'Heinz Hot Soups', 1970

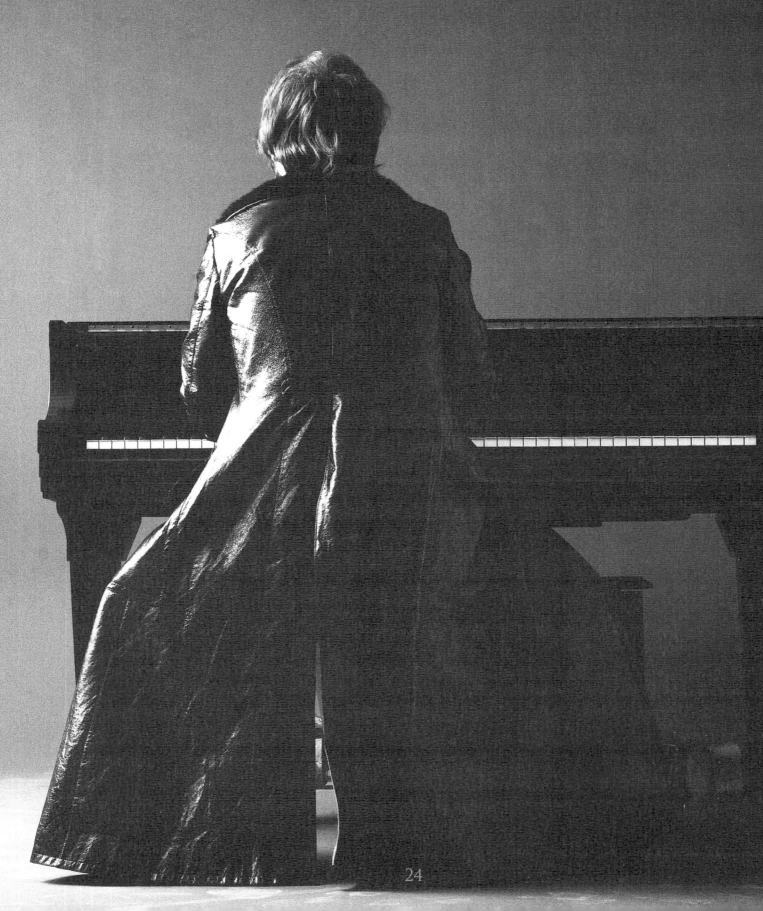

'OK…I've never been in nor do I know where 20 Denmark Street is, so I can only assume it is where Elton (then Reg Dwight) worked as a gopher for Mills Music. The problem here is that Elton worked there in this capacity three years before we were introduced. He was already a professional musician by the time we met in '67. As for the sitting on the roof bit, fanciful icing on the cake, I imagine. Believe me, nobody back then would have allowed some unfamiliar teenage friend of the tea boy to be perched precariously on their roof scribbling away like some hayseed Byron, romantic imagery, indeed."

But despite its humble beginnings on a kitchen table, the song remains one of Elton's most famous and adored recordings. However, it was not chosen as the single. Instead the more upbeat Border Song was released and Elton got to perform it on the BBC's behemoth music show *'Top of the Pops'*, which attracted some 15 million viewers each week.

Once again the single failed to chart, but at least this time the album did, selling 10,000 copies and earning rave reviews. But neither DJM, nor Elton himself wanted to be *'cultish'* and only appreciated by fellow musicians and music journalists.

It was decided that the only way to develop Elton's appeal and get that yearned for hit single was to go out on the road.

A band was put together, including Nigel Olsson and Dee Murray, and off they went. Elton was nervous at first, but saw the sense in the plan. Within weeks he had warmed up on stage and began to deliver more engaging performances supporting the Pretty Things and T Rex among others.

As DJM had contacts in America it was decided to release Border Song over there. Although it only entered the lower end of the Billboard Top 100 it did well enough to win Elton a deal and get the album in front of Russ Regan at Universal. Russ loved the album and said he would release it if Elton came to America on a promotional tour.

'I thought it was one of the greatest pieces of music I'd ever heard in my life,' he said. *'We have to break him here in America'.*

So Dick James was persuaded to fund one last attempt to launch Elton John.

The idea of an unknown piano player with a small band undertaking an American concert tour came from left field. But of course it was too tempting to ignore, despite Elton's reservations that the band was too new to go transatlantic.

But Elton was used to life on the road so off he went. Although his hopes were high, his expectations were low.

The American team set up to promote Elton had organized a week at a well-known Los Angeles club called The Troubadour. The club's owner Doug Weston was prepared to take a risk on the unknown piano player after hearing, and loving, the Elton John album.

The scene in LA at that time was still vibrant as it transitioned from the groovy 1960s.

After Elton took to the stage for his American debut on August 25, 1970, introduced by Neil Diamond he managed a transition of his own. All the experience he had gained from life on the road and

Elton John Portrait, 1970

backing a succession of experienced artists came together for him. His performance was incredible. Giving it his all, he seemed almost possessed as he threw back his head, pounded his piano and rocked out, exhorting the audience to join in. By all accounts it was an electrifying performance, which he would repeat each evening in a landmark six-night residency. He had a ball. The set list included: Sixty Years On, I Need You To Turn To, Border Song, Take Me To the Pilot, Honky Tonk Woman, Country Comfort and Burn Down the Mission. Several tracks, including the last two on this list, were from his third album Tumbleweed Connection which had been written but not yet released.

Watched by the great and the good of the LA music scene, Elton's show is rated by Rolling Stone magazine as among the 50 greatest concerts of the last 50 years. It was not just career changing — it was life changing. Elton was simply sensational.

After the first night, Robert Hilburn, music critic for the Los Angeles Times, wrote: *'Tuesday night at the Troubadour was just the beginning. He's going to be one of rock's biggest and most important stars.'*

'That one night and one review saved me a year's work,' Elton said later. *'Right place, right time; luck.'*

Word spread there was a new star in town —audiences clamoured for tickets and among the famous names to witness this dynamic debut were Mike Love of The Beach Boys, 3 Dog Night and Quincy Jones. Most exciting of all for Elton was when his idol American musician and songwriter Leon Russell dropped by.

After being treated with kindness and respect by musicians, including Leon, whom he had admired for years, his confidence grew.

• • • • ⟶

Elton John performs at Doug Weston's Troubadour on August 25, 1970 in Los Angeles

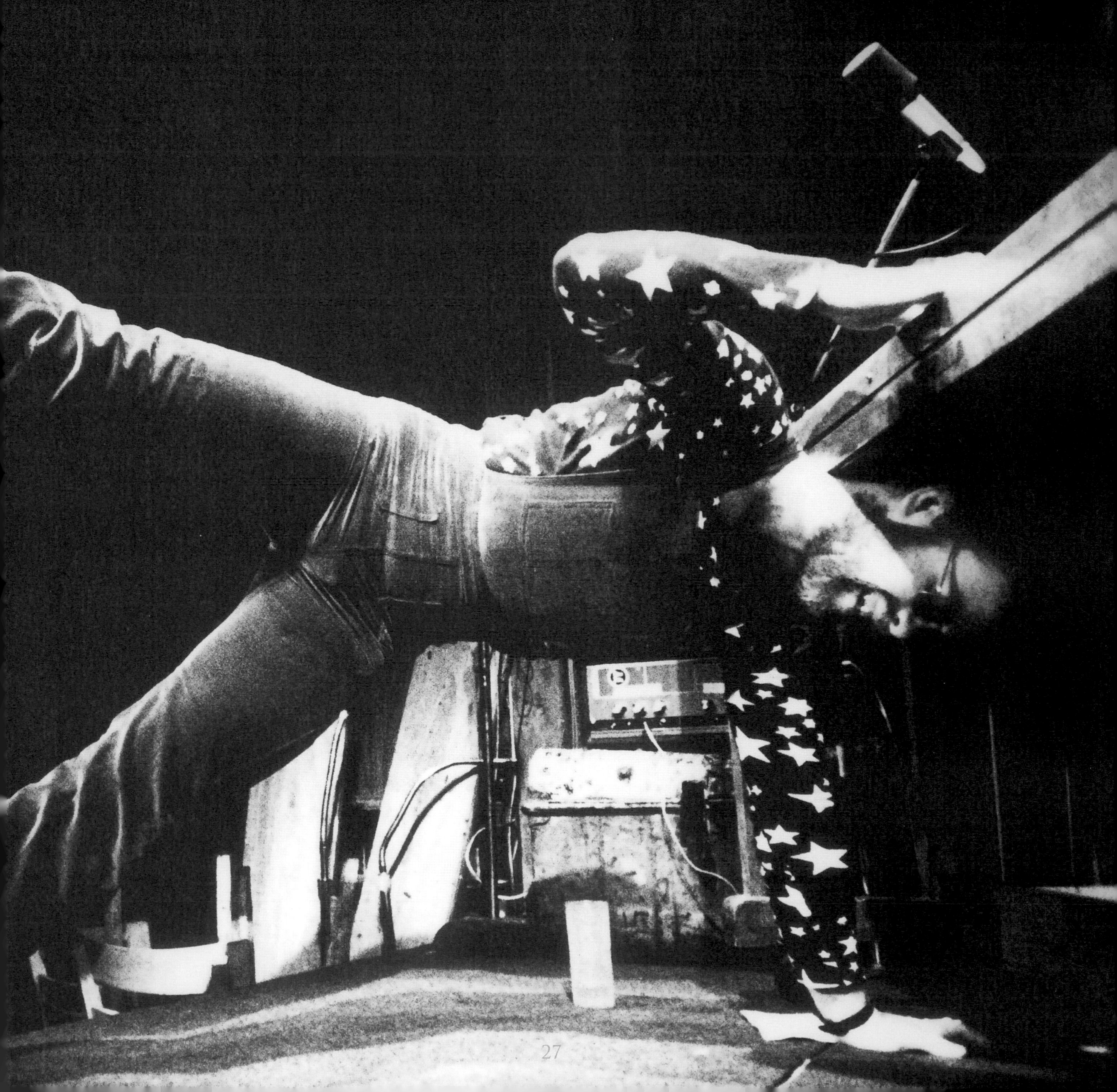

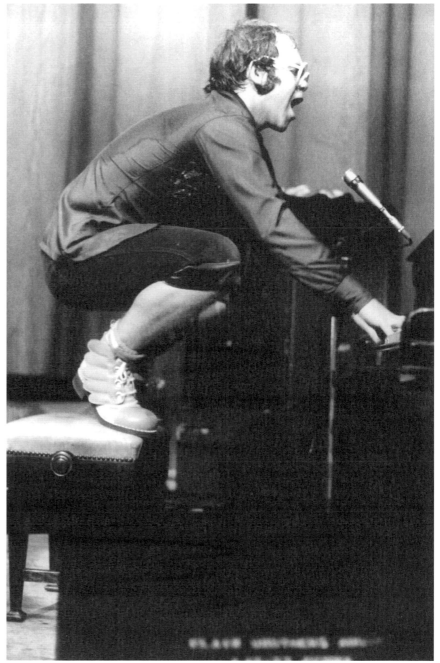

↑ L: Elton John relaxes backstage at Doug Weston's
Troubadour on August 25, 1970 in Los Angeles

↑ R: Elton John standing on his piano stool during a
performance in 1971

• • • • ──────────────────────────────→

Image from Vogue 1971

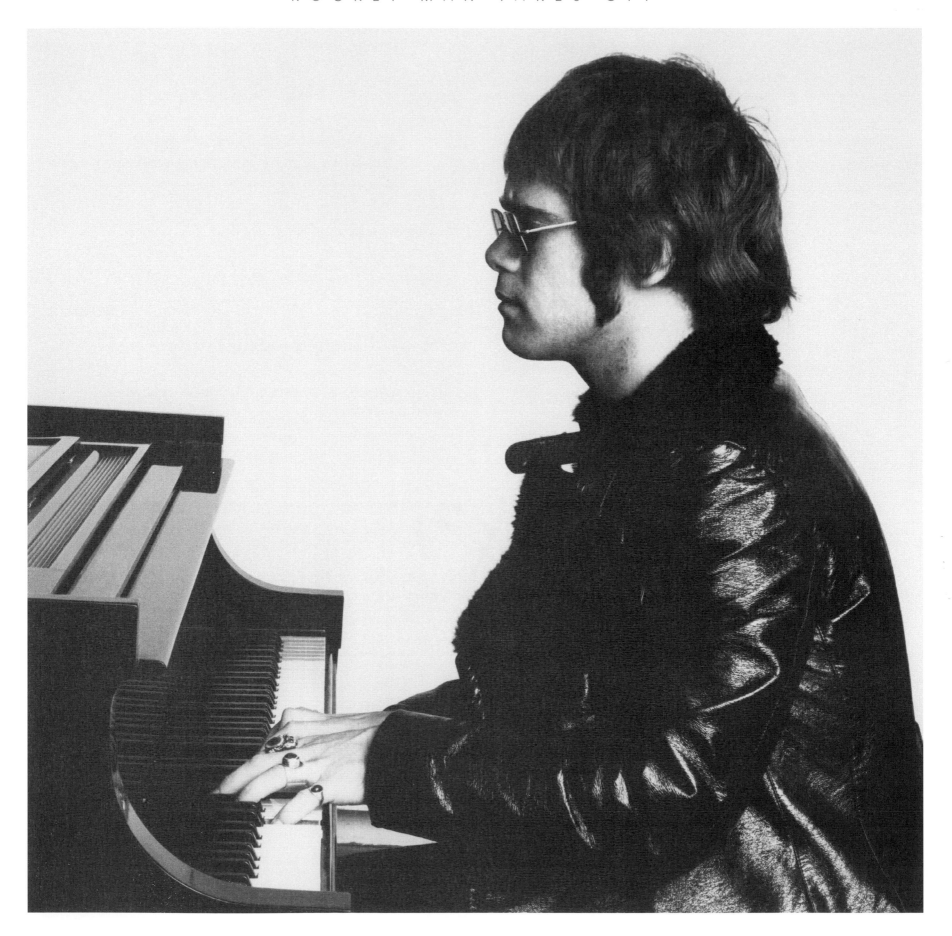

'Everything I loved about music came from America,' said Elton looking back on that time in his later years. *'So when you come here and meet your idols — wow'.*

By the **beginning of** September 1970, sales of the Elton John album were **topping** 30,000 copies.

With so many acts having tried and failed to crack America in the past, Elton didn't imagine that he would return to the UK having done it. The Beatles had led the British Invasion of 1964 but in many ways the American music scene was largely self-sufficient. Certainly a bespectacled piano player seemed an unlikely candidate to be the next transatlantic phenomenon.

So when he and Bernie returned to England in the autumn, that triumph must have seemed like a dream as little appeared to have changed for them back home at first.

Long before social media would spread news in real time, the story of his stonking triumph in LA was slow to reach the UK. When Elton fulfilled his commitment to back Fotheringay, a short-lived British folk rock group, at the Royal Albert Hall in early October 1970 he was still largely unknown in his homeland.

The only hint that things were beginning to change for him was when he took to the stage wearing a gold lame coat in the style of Busby Berkeley which he had picked up in America — oh and the fact that he stole the show every night of course.

He and Bernie went back to live with Sheila and Fred, picking up their life in London while they awaited the release of their third album Tumbleweed Connection. Amazingly in the short meantime Elton and Bernie also wrote and recorded another album *'Friends'* the

Elton John performing on stage at the Crystal Palace Bowl in London, England on July 31, 1971

sound track to a Lewis Gilbert teen movie of the same name. The work had been commissioned before Elton's success in the States. Although he and Bernie dutifully fulfilled their promise to do the job, the songs were evidently hurried and the album isn't really representative of their overall canon of work.

Tumbleweed Connection is an altogether superior album, having been largely completed before the US tour. Again it was produced and arranged by Gus Dudgeon and Paul Buckmaster, but with a different, more country, less grandiose style than the Elton John album. The arrangements were toned down and Bernie's lyrics, this time about the American West, and Elton's voice were more to the fore.

Once again, acclaim in the UK came from music critics and industry worthies, rather than from record-buying fans and there were no hit singles from the album. But this piece of Americana was perfect for the new fan base across the water. Bernie had always loved the Wild West — soaking up the films and atmosphere as a child in Lincolnshire home. As before, the audience was more appreciative in America, where the album went to number five in the Billboard Hot 100 chart.

So the sensible course of action was to get Elton back to the States to ride the wave and capitalise on his success. A full-scale tour was quickly arranged and Elton set off in November to perform in large auditoriums in his own right for the first time, taking in cities including Chicago and New York.

This tour saw Elton truly come into his own. Having once accidentally knocked over his piano stool to audience approval, he repeated the act purposely in future performances. His extrovert performances saw him squatting and clambering around on the piano, wearing increasingly outlandish and garishly coloured costumes, accessorised with hats and glasses that grew more absurd. The inner showman was loose.

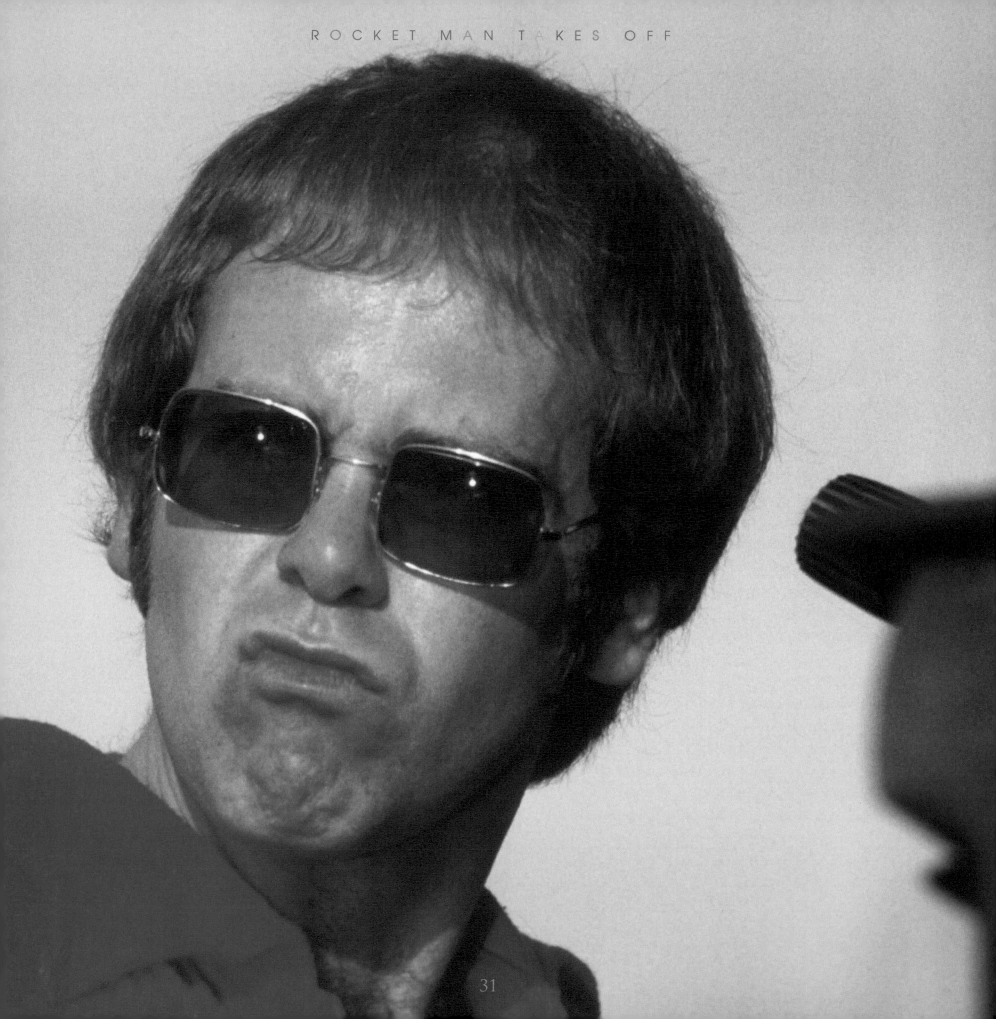

His stage presence had grown. While the apparent personality change from shy boy to showman seemed inexplicable to many of those around him then, Elton himself offered the most reasonable explanation years later; *'I was escaping the repression of my childhood'*, he says. *'I lived my teenage years in my 20s and when I got successful all hell broke loose.*

'For 23 years I had led a very sheltered life', he told an American chat show in 1980. *'I was always told what to do as a child. And I didn't have much of a teenage life — I wasn't allowed to wear winkle pickers or even Hush Puppies. Then suddenly I was boss and having a ball. Wham bam, thank you mam, suddenly everything was fantastic.'*

Another big change around this time was the departure of Ray Williams as his *'personal manager'*. Although he'd been so influential in launching Elton, Ray was still merely an employee at DJM, where Dick James was not enamoured with his work. Ray himself could see the writing on the wall and agreed that Elton needed different management now his career was taking off. Although the eventual sudden manner of his departure is described as being rather a brutal severance of his contract, it is unclear whether Elton was aware of the detail of what went on as by then he was miles away on his American concert tour.

A live concert in New York on November 17 was recorded and released as a live album; 11-17-70 (the date in the American style with month first).

Elton is on record as saying that he believes 11-17-70 to be his best live performance recording and cites the album as being a great showcase for band members Nigel Olsson and Dee Murray.

By now Your Song had been released as a single in America and it made the top 40 during Elton's tour. By January 1971 it would reach

number eight and this pushed Elton's team in London to release it in the UK in their ongoing quest for a British hit single. That is how, one year and one month after its release as an album track, Your Song at last exploded into the UK top 10 in early February 1971. At last Elton, and Bernie, got the recognition they had always yearned for.

All this information on chart positions, together with other facts and figures such as concert audience sizes and takings, would be recorded by Elton afterward as he continued with his childhood habit of making meticulous notes about the minutiae of his day. He also remained an avid pop fan and toured American record shops to add to his already enormous collection. He was living proof of Aristotle's philosophical words; *'Give me a child until he is seven and I will show you the man'*.

There was no doubt that a dazzling career was launched — but it was on a rather haphazard trajectory. There was no real plan, nor any control. This resulted in overkill, most clearly evidenced by the fact that at one stage in 1970 there were four Elton John albums in the shops at the same time.

Elton desperately needed someone to steer and ground him.

Enter John Reid, a young, rather suave, Glaswegian who by the age of 19 had worked his way up through the music industry to become the UK manager of EMI's soul label, Tamla Motown. John and Elton had moved in similar circles on the London music scene but it wasn't until John Reid's 21st birthday that the pair would hook up at one of Elton's gigs in San Francisco. They got on famously. John was urbane and astute, with great business acumen. Within just a few weeks Elton decided that he wanted him as his new manager.

• • • • ──────────────────────────▶

Portrait of Elton John backstage at the Crystal Palace Garden Party, London, 31st July 1971

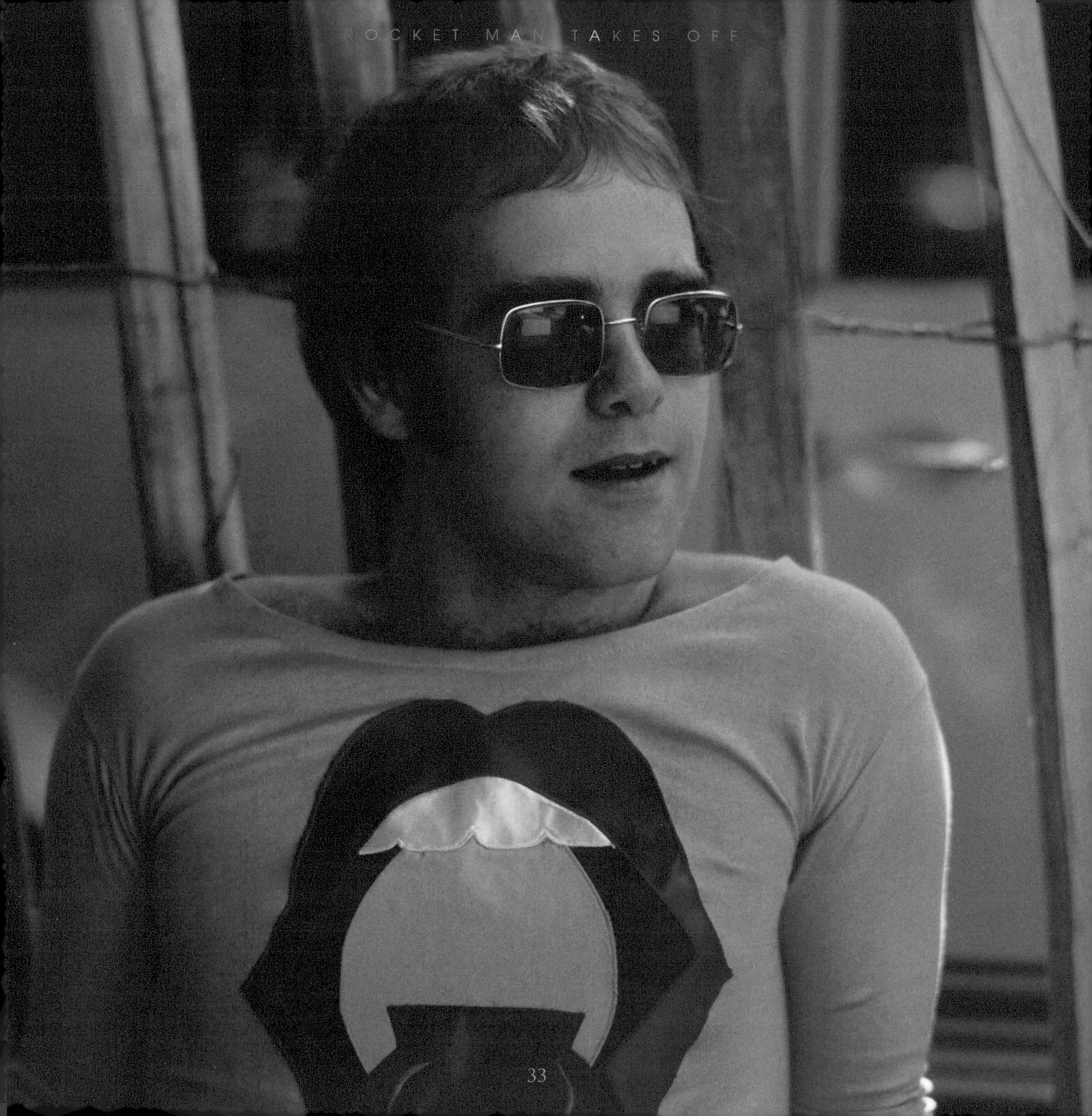

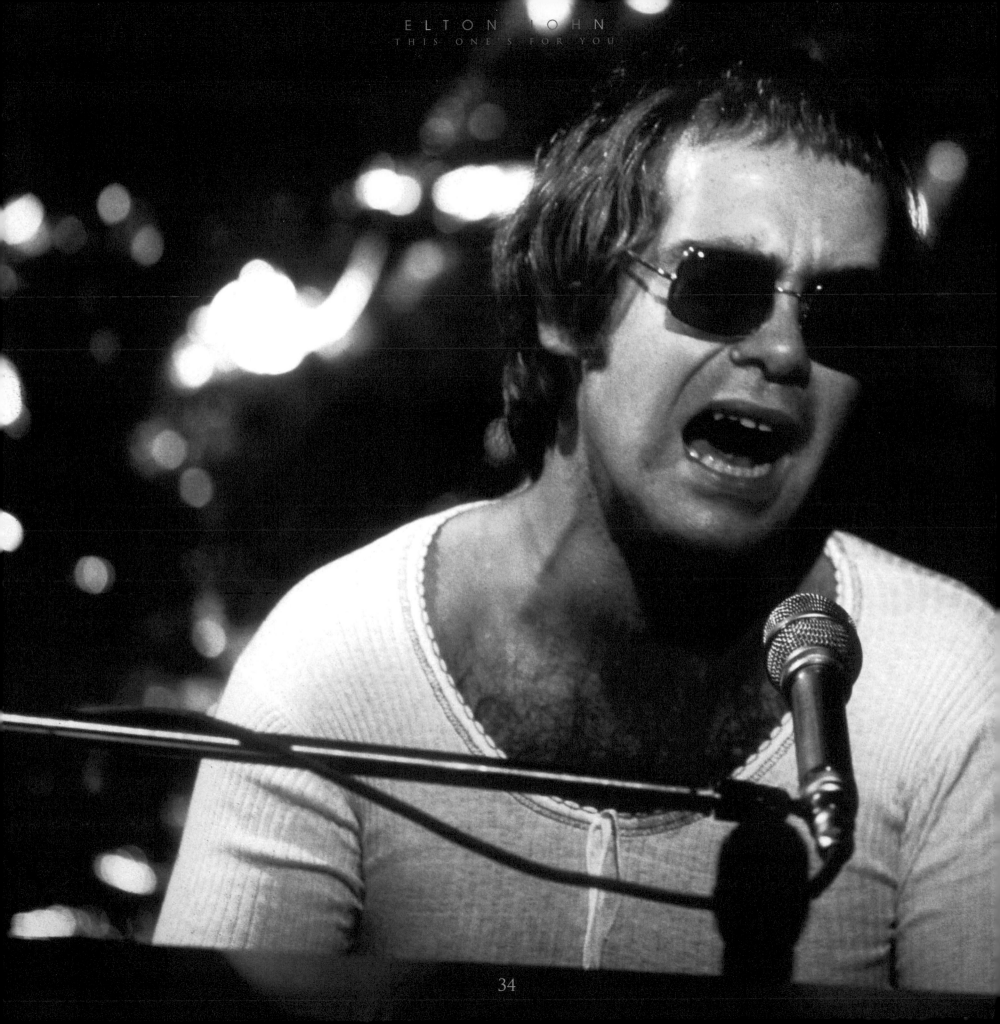

The two men were also an item romantically for a while and moved in together to a new apartment in Water Gardens, London.

Although Elton had had close friendships with men before, including sharing a room with Bernie, those had always been platonic. But things were different with John Reid and so Elton came out to his immediate circle, including Sheila and Fred who took the news well. They liked John and were pleased that Elton had found happiness.

The fact the John was in Elton's life 24/7 was a bonus. Elton was exhausted following the frenetic round of touring and transatlantic trips and was exhibiting the first signs of the tantrums and emotional outbursts which would come to be part of the 'legend'.

In his new role as Elton's manager, John could protect and chaperone him at home and abroad. Having worked in the business for years he was well used to checking contracts and publishing agreements and managing the money. John was to look after Elton in the same way that his mother, grandmother and aunt had done back in Pinner when he was young. Elton was closely guided and guarded by John, in the manner that his new role of 'rock star on the rise' demanded.

In 1971 came the fourth studio album, the haunting 'Madman Across The Water' including the talents of session musicians such as Rick Wakeman. Writing about the album for '1000 Albums You Must Hear Before You Die' music journalist John Tobler said; ' Unsurprisingly, given Wakeman's involvement, there is a whiff of prog rock about the proceedings, while Paul Buckmaster's lush string arrangements serve to further expand the sound'.

The layered orchestrations were part of a clear effort to repeat the success of the Elton John album. The attempt was further enhanced by the fact that Elton and Bernie had clearly matured as songwriters — both able to draw on their real life experiences in America. Bernie had now seen for himself the country of his childhood dreams and Elton had improved his skills as a singer and performer.

Yet, despite the best efforts of everyone involved, the album failed to cause a stir in the UK where there was still no chart breakthrough. It did ok in America however, reaching number eight in the album chart and spawning the singles Tiny Dancer and Levon which were Top 40 hits.

Despite reports that he considered giving it all up, Elton gathered himself to go into 1972. In January 1972 he made his stage name of Elton John his new legal name; changing it by deed poll and adding the middle name Hercules — perhaps a clear statement that he had the strength of character to carry on.

Marc Bolan of T-Rex performing with Elton John on the BBC television show Top of the Pops on December 20, 1971

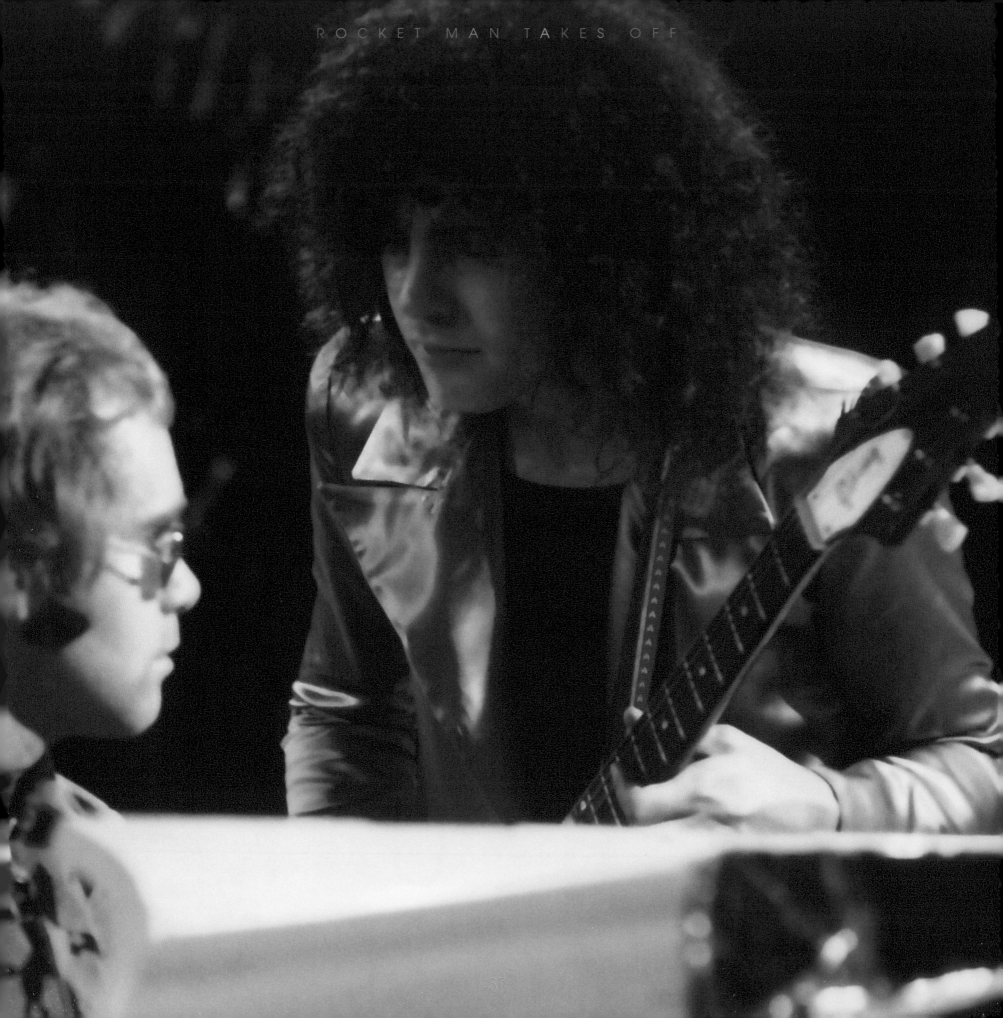

CHAPTER FOUR

THE CLASSIC YEARS AND GOLDEN RUN OF ALBUMS

1972 - 75

Elton desperately needed to build on the momentum around him and his next, and seventh, album Honky Château was the one that did it, launching Elton John into the pop and rock stratosphere.

The landscape in which Elton launched Honky Château in the UK was glittering to say the least. In 1972 the UK was dominated by the music and fashions of the glam rock movement — characterised by musicians wearing flamboyant and outrageous costumes, make up and glitter.

Generally accepted as having begun with Marc Bolan and T. Rex the previous year, the genre was now at its peak with pretty, pouting, preening pop stars appearing on the nation's screens week after week on Top of the Pops.

Although he jumped in with the glam rockers, Elton was not really like them — other than in his love for a platform boot and a stonking rhythm. He quickly recognised that he could not compete on level terms with the kohl-eyed sensuality of Marc Bolan, nor the gender-bending appeal and avante garde leanings of David Bowie. So he needed another angle.

In real life he was a witty man who could reduce his friends and colleagues to tears of laughter. Elton decided to bring that sense of the comedic to his image and performances. He mocked himself, before anyone else could do it, staring sardonically at the camera. It is hard to send up someone who gets there before you.

But behind all the stage shenanigans and posturing is a body of work that has ensured Elton's place in the annals of pop and rock forever more. And it all began with Honky Château.

Released in 1972, Honky Château was recorded in the 17th century Château d'Hérouville, in northern France. Offering 10 bedrooms, a pool, a tennis court and expansive grounds of parkland, the studio was popular with many stars and bands during the 1970s. Being just 25 miles north of Paris it was conveniently close enough to the French capital for Elton's off duty hours to be spent happily exploring the city's many fashion shops.

The album was made during a golden time for Elton and Bernie's song-writing partnership, when everything came together. Armed with Bernie's words and ideas, Elton worked fast and effectively.

The long, more complex songs were ditched in favour of shorter numbers and were more 'pop' in style, with simpler arrangements.

Critically, the album is regarded as one of Elton and Bernie's most accomplished works — reaching number two in the UK album charts and spending five weeks at number one in the US.

Its eclectic track list contained two hit singles, Rocket Man and Honky Cat. And Rocket Man was the single that out-charted Your Song and made Elton an international star.

Using the same production team and theme of astronaut alone in space which had been so successful in 1969-70 for David Bowie with 'Space Oddity', the song went to number two in the UK (and number six in the US).

But it wasn't a copy of Bowie's song. The Apollo human spaceflight and exploration programme was still huge news in 1972, just three years after the first moon landing. So the topic was still current and also worked well as an analogy comparing the isolation of a pop star from the real world, with the isolation of an astronaut above the earth.

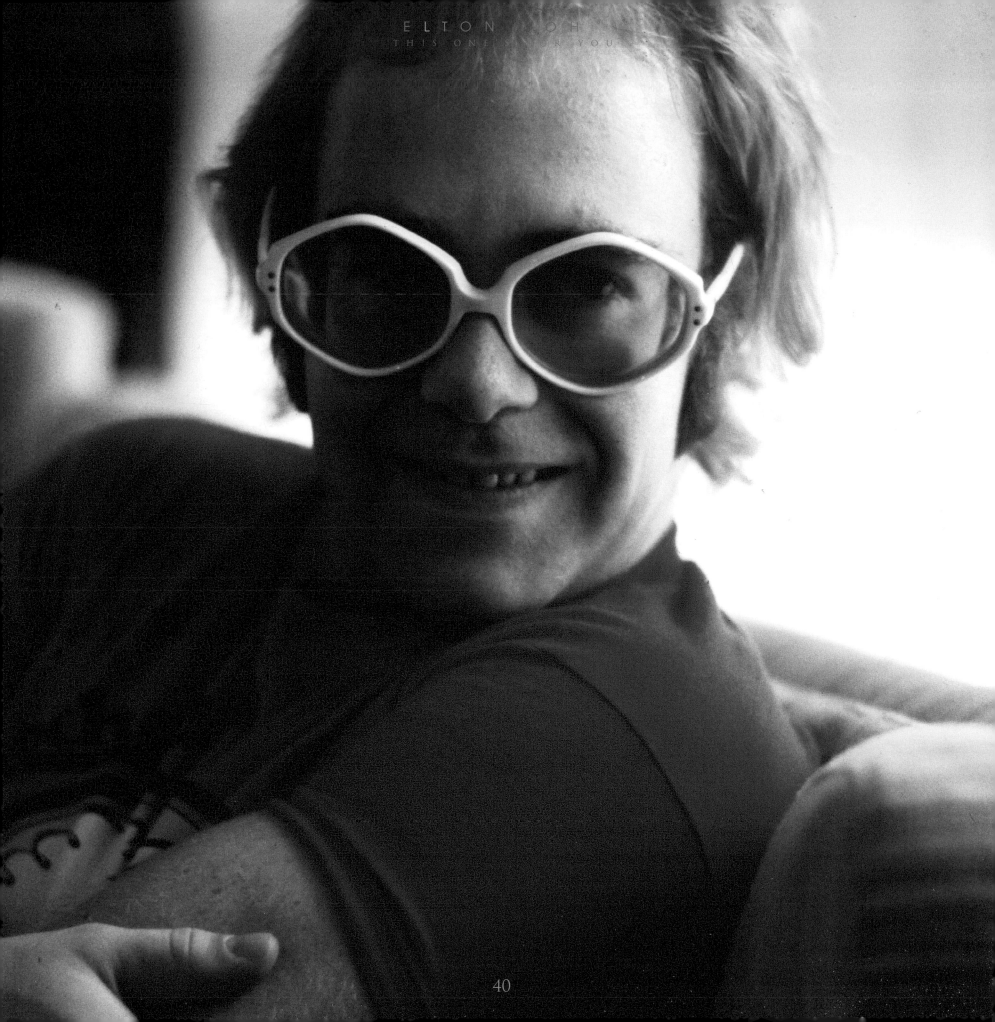

The technology in pop had changed too and the modern synthesizer and slide guitars were both used to eerie effect on this recording by producer Gus Dudgeon. The lyric, *'I'm a rocket man....'* is accompanied by an ascending slide guitar roll which simulates the sound of a *'lift off'*.

And as on Your Song, Elton begins singing in an almost conversational style, *'She packed my bags last night, preflight'.*

The song and album was also important in heralding a change to Elton's band. Up until now he had still been operating as a trio with Nigel Olsson on drums and Dee Murray on bass guitar. But producer Gus Dudgeon wanted a fuller sound for the studio and brought in additional musicians, including, pivotally, Davey Johnstone on lead guitar, mandolin and banjo. *'It shifted the momentum once I started writing with guitars in mind and the hits started to come',* Elton has acknowledged since.

With the original Elton John album, Tumbleweed Connection, Madman Across the Water and now Honky Château all having achieved platinum sales in America, Elton was now the biggest rock star in that country.

But it was the success of Honky Château and particularly Rocket Man in the UK that was the icing on the cake. Elton was overjoyed to triumph in his homeland at last and on the back of it he undertook his first major tour of the UK in 1972. It was quite a sensation. He went at it at full pelt, dressed garishly with coloured hair and multi-coloured, embroidered and monogrammed costumes fashioned in satin and quilts — everything was completely over the top. He was determined to give his fans value for money and make an impact upon them in the same way that the 1950s rockers he had enjoyed, like Little Richard, had made an impact on him.

His performances were incredible — incorporating elements of

the vaudeville and pantomime he had known as a child. He was now combining his virtuoso piano-playing skills with a performance to rival the wildman of guitar Jimi Hendrix. But unlike Hendrix he couldn't throw his instrument around — *'It's a 9ft plank that you have to make interesting'* he says.

So he did everything but swing it around — he coloured it, bejeweled it, played it with his feet and his fists, put his legs on it, did handstands on it, crawled under it, clambered over it and at times seemed to almost levitate to be on a level with it. In short he transcended and transformed piano playing, even eclipsing the showman from his childhood years, Liberace.

Elton appeared to love his new found and well-earned success. He took it all in his stride and became this wild crazy character, larger than life and funny. When his antics and costumes didn't really suit the mood of the song, Bernie may have raised an eyebrow, but he basically let it go. Elton says it is largely to Bernie's credit that the pair of them have never fallen out.

His work ethic was undimmed by all the theatrics. He continued to work with other artists and around this time set up his own label, Rocket Records that was mostly focused on new talent — most famously the singer Kiki Dee.

But in the meantime the albums kept coming and the hits started to flow. His ninth studio offering was Don't Shoot Me I'm Only the Piano Player issued in early 1973, again recorded at Château d'Hérouville and produced by Gus Dudgeon whose wide-ranging ability to produce different sounding recordings really did justice to such a diverse collection of songs. Gus possessed stellar skills and made a major contribution to Elton's success. Many commentators believe him to be as important to Elton as George Martin was to the Beatles. He produced all Elton's classic albums of the early 1970s.

← ———————————————————— • • • •

Elton John at his home in Windsor, United Kingdom, 1972

↑ Elton John in a flamboyant stage outfit of white suit with
feather trim and rhinestone encrusted glasses, circa 1973

Elton John at his home in Wentworth, Surrey, during a
shoot for the cover of 'Elton John's Greatest Hits', 1974

Including the legendary tracks Daniel and Crocodile Rock which both became monumental hit singles, Don't Shoot Me I'm Only the Piano Player confirmed Elton's star status. It gave him his first number one in the UK and also topped the album charts in America and Australia.

Elton was now making big money — and showing a flair for spending it. He moved with John Reid to a swanky home in the exclusive area of Virginia Water, Surrey, in spring 1972. He also began to acquire art, to add to his collection of records, augmented by a jukebox, and start new collections of objet d'art, posters, pop art, games and clothes. Then there were the cars — from Aston Martins to Rolls Royce's — the dinky toys collection of his childhood had been replaced by real vehicles.

His pace of work never let up and just a few months later, in October, he launched his masterpiece album, — Goodbye Yellow Brick Road. Many consider this to be the best album he ever made. It has sold more than 30 million copies ensuring Elton's place in the music history books.

Elton had wanted to record this album in Jamaica, but encountered countless difficulties with the studio on arrival. So in the end he and the entourage decamped back to France and the Strawberry Studios within Château d'Hérouville. But during the hiatus while things were being sorted out, Elton and Bernie were holed up in a hotel in Kingston, Jamaica and — proving that every cloud has a silver lining — composed 21 songs in three days. They had enough strong songs for a double album.

Elton always worked quickly when given Bernie's lyrics, apparently spending only around half an hour, and never more than an hour, on any one composition.

With 17 songs across four sides, Goodbye Yellow Brick Road includes four mega-hit singles. It could easily have been four more but for the fact that music managers of the time believed that releasing too many tracks as singles meant the kiss of death for album sales.

Some of Elton's best-loved songs are here, including — as well as the rousing title track — Bennie and the Jets, Saturday Night's Alright For Fighting, Funeral for a Friend/Love Lies Bleeding and the tribute to Marilyn Monroe, Candle in the Wind.

A novel and grandiose mix of ballads and rock and roll — truly the weird and the wonderful as referenced in the Bennie and the Jets lyrics — its unabashed pure pop sound garnered instant acclaim from critics and fans alike and the album topped the charts in the UK and the US.

On top of creating these classic albums, Elton didn't let up on the touring.

Glam rockers were still going strong — and Elton was firmly established among their number. In the glam rock tradition he even made a fun Christmas record, Step Into Christmas' with a B-side called Ho, Ho, Ho (Who'd Be a Turkey at Christmas).

His ostentatious costumes fitted the moment perfectly — nothing was too over the top. Whether dressed as Donald Duck or a mad Mardi Gras-style cockerel, or decked out in feather or banana epaulettes, or wearing spikey, brightly coloured wigs and heavy feathered and bejeweled head dresses, Elton made an entrance like no other and his live performances were not to be missed.

His concerts were like parties. His audiences were liberally studded with major celebrities.

Elton John performing live, 1973

44

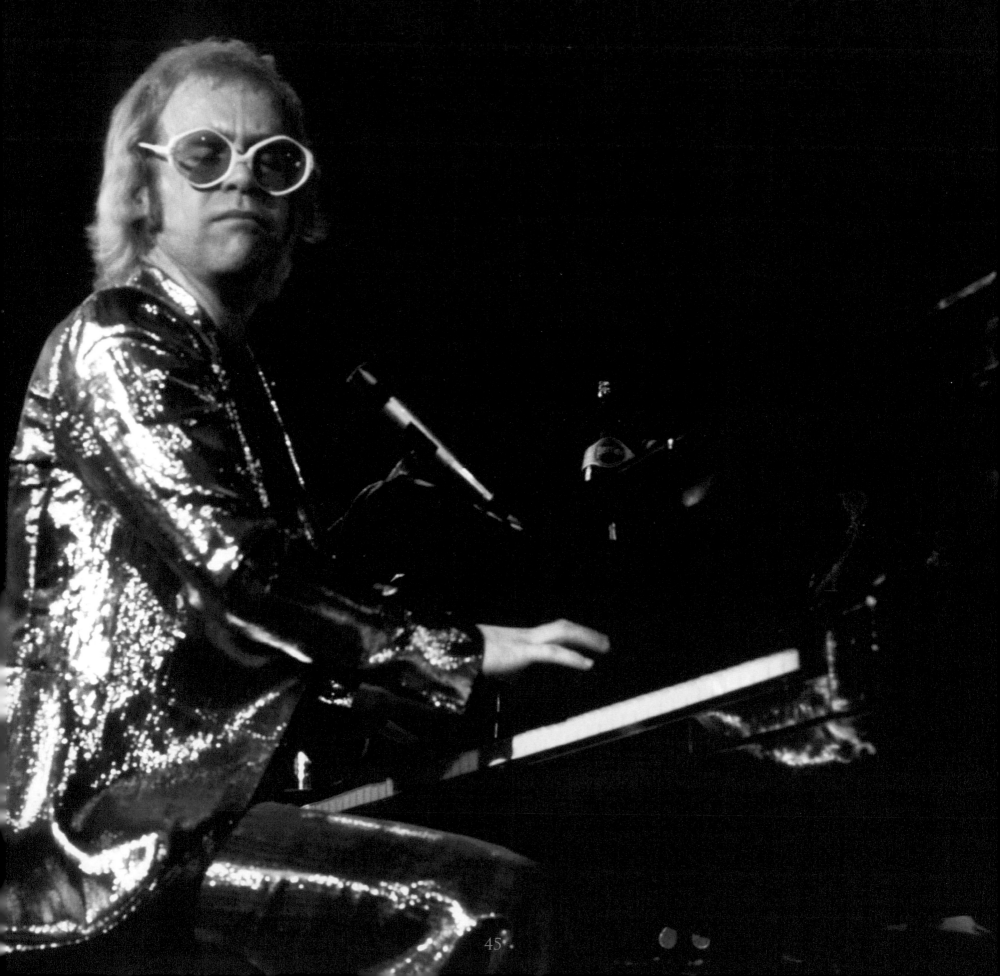

Based behind his piano Elton could not move around the stage and reach out to his audience in the way that vocalists and guitarists can do. So costumes were vital in making sure that he was the centre of attention on stage. They also provided a type of armour, strengthening his stage persona.

'I was never a sex symbol so I had fun with my outfits and just went for it', says Elton. *'Critics said it took away from integrity and maybe it did. I took it too far, but that's what an addict does'.*

Then there were the trademark glasses, which he had in all shapes and sizes and adorned with everything from feathers and fluff to palm trees and windscreen wipers — many from LA optician to the stars Dennis Roberts. According to People magazine in 1975, Elton had spent US$25,000 on glasses alone; *'a dazzling spectrum ranging from simple rhinestone-encrusted star shapes to a US$5,000 extravaganza spelling 'ELTON' in 57 battery-operated flashing mini-bulbs'.*

Elton has since described using glasses as helping to overcome the fact that he was actually shy and self-conscious. They became props to hide behind so that he didn't have to look people in the eye.

His love of a platform boot is similarly well documented in photographs of the time. Outrageous platform boots regularly boosted his 5ft 8-inch frame — strangely enough his great grandfather William Dwight had been a shoemaker in Buckinghamshire.

These costumes and theatrics endeared him to fans young and old. With so few television and radio channels at the time, parents and children were often together watching and listened to the same music. And of course he wasn't a sexy or unsettling performer in the style of Bowie or Freddie Mercury of Queen, which had became one of the most popular bands in the world in the mid-'70s.

So he set his stall around music as entertainment, rather than the art to which Bowie — his contemporary and fellow escapee from the London suburbs — pursued. The irony around these two men was that while Bowie flirted with the gay community while married to a woman, Elton was actually gay and living with a man, yet would not bring this aspect of his life to the public's attention for many years to come.

In the meantime, he enjoyed a certain boy- next-door appeal and kept his relationship with John Reid a secret from the general public, although it was known in the industry and among his own circle. During a tour in early 1973 he enjoyed the same level of adulation and high pitched screaming as more conventional *'crushes'* such as teeny bopper idols The Osmonds and David Cassidy.

His appeal was truly cross-generational and knew no class barriers. Fans even included the Queen mother whom he got to know having been friendly with the Queen's sister, Princess Margaret after meeting her at a benefit concert.

Speaking on the Graham Norton chat show years later he recounted how once when he was dancing with Princess Anne at Prince Andrew's 21st birthday party the Queen came over asked to join them. *'We danced to Bill Haley's Rock Around the Clock. It was one of the most surreal moments of my life — having been born in a council house in Pinner.'*

Other close friends of his at the time included Surrey neighbours Bryan Forbes, the film director and his actress wife Nanette Newman. Elton trusted Bryan enough to allow him to make a documentary chronicling a year of his life, including the writing and recording of Goodbye Yellow Brick Road. Entitled *'Elton John and Bernie Taupin Say Goodbye Norma Jean and Other Things'* it was released in 1973.

Elton John performing live, 1973

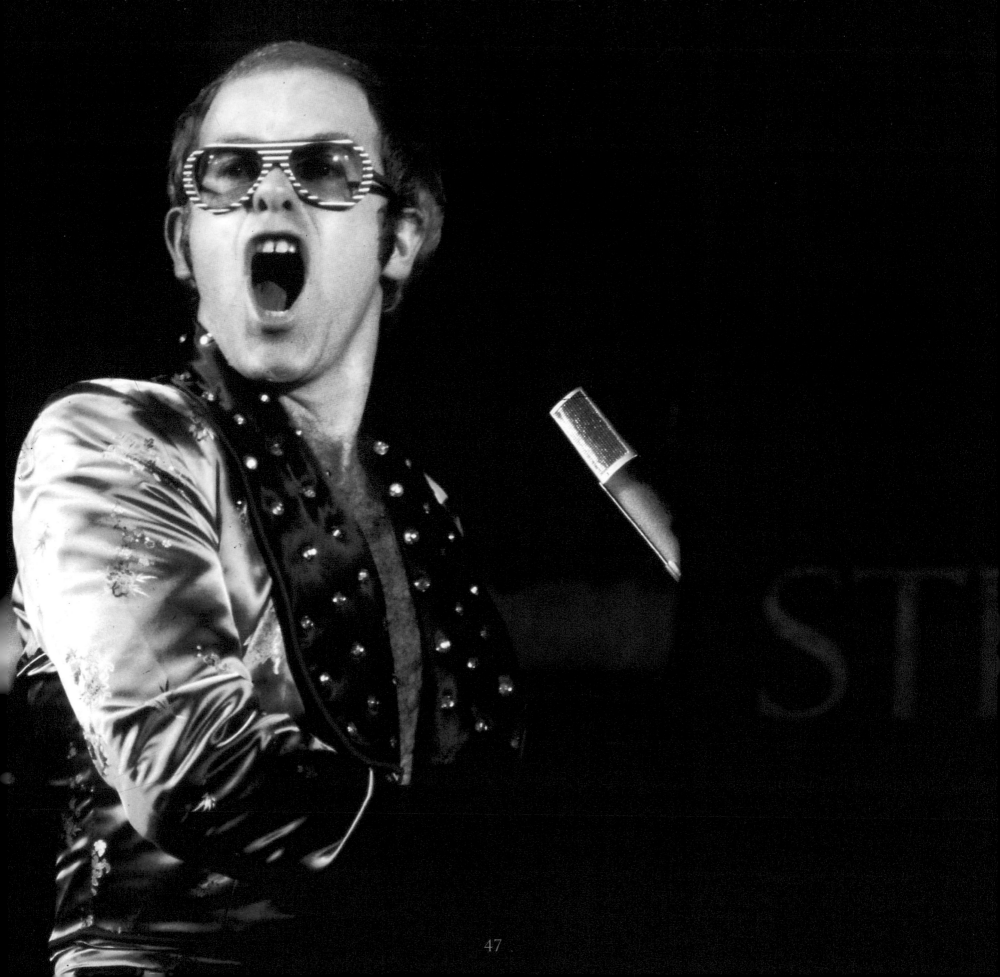

Bryan's introduction to the film captured the many contradictions in Elton's character as follows:

'A child with every toy in the shop and not a key to wind them with ... as much an enigma to himself as to his friends ....now possessing no inhibitions, now totally inhibited... seeking fame one minute, determined to reject it the next.... jealous of his privacy, hating to be private....arrogant, contrite, gifted, lonely ...the superstar who does his own hoovering.'

By now Elton's own record label, The Rocket Record Company, was busy signing up artists. The label was launched in early 1973 and its directors were Elton, Bernie, John Reid, Gus Dudgeon and Steve Brown.

Elton pledged, on the front cover of the leading weekly music magazine Melody Maker that *'What we are offering is undivided love and devotion, a f*****g good royalty for the artist and a company that works its b*****ks off.'* He wanted to foster new artists, particularly at that time his guitarist Davey Johnstone, so he didn't record on it himself.

Even when he was out of that contract in 1975 he chose to sign a contract with the American recording company MCA (he had been on their smaller label, Uni, run by Russ Regan before this). MCA released a greatest hits album Elton John's Greatest Hits which went to number one on both sides of the Atlantic in 1974. It is certified Diamond by the RIAA in the states for selling 16 million copies.

The follow up to Goodbye Yellow Brick Road was his eighth studio album Caribou, also released in 1974, giving Elton his third number one in the UK and topping the charts in the US, Canada and Australia.

Another fast recording, reportedly made in less than a fortnight sandwiched in between concerts to fulfill contractual obligations, it

included hit singles, The Bitch is Back and Don't Let The Sun Go Down On Me.

By now Bernie was married to Maxine Feibelman who he had met in America and it is she who is frequently credited with inspiring Bernie to write this after she used the phrase *'I see the bitch is back'*, when Elton got into one of his famous *'moods'*.

Despite a truly grueling work schedule, Elton remained in fine voice. The vocals on Caribou are sublime. But it wasn't truly an equal to the colossus that was Goodbye Yellow Brick Road. However in the eyes of the record-buying public Elton and his band could do no wrong so it was still a big success. It was the best-selling album of 1975 in the United States and went on to sell more than 10 million copies.

In the notes to the 1995 CD re-release, Elton describes being *'under enormous pressure'* to finish the album before leaving for a tour of Japan. Even its name is simply a nod to the Colorado Caribou Ranch studios where it was recorded.

Producer Gus Dudgeon added backing vocals, and finishing touches after the band had left the studio. Elton famously never enjoyed being in the studio so would generally leave as soon as he had laid down his vocals and piano.

His tour of North America in 1974 — the eighth in just four years — was his biggest yet. He did 45 concerts 31 cities in 70 days. A private jet was the only way of maintaining such pace over vast distances. Like everything else in Elton's life at the time, his jet — a Boeing 720 called The Starship — was incredible. The custom design included a fake fireplace and a bar fitted with an electric organ.

• • • • ⟶

Elton John on stage at Hawaii International Center, Honolulu, Hawaii, October 1974

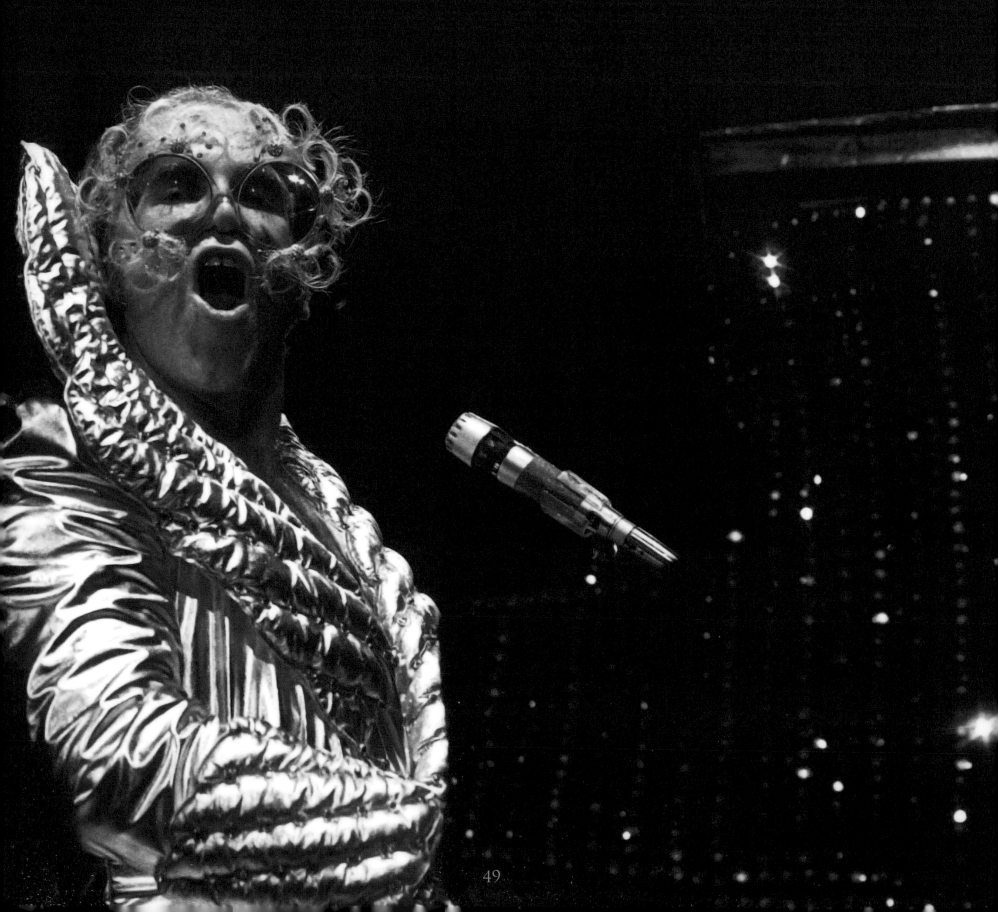

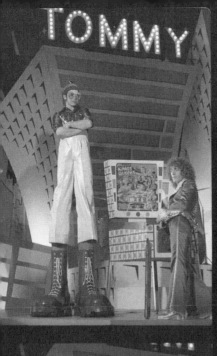
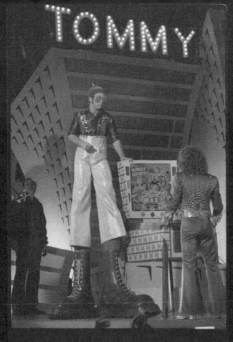
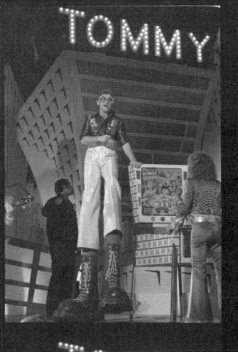
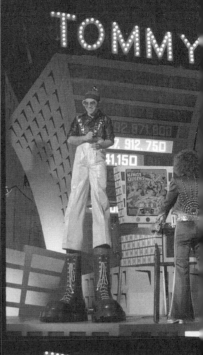
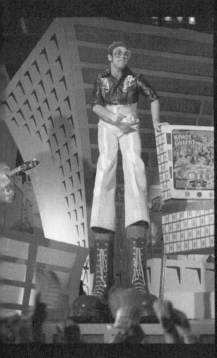
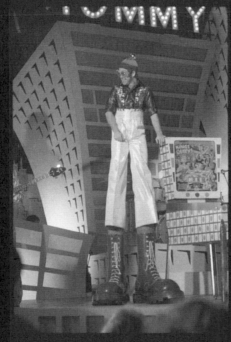
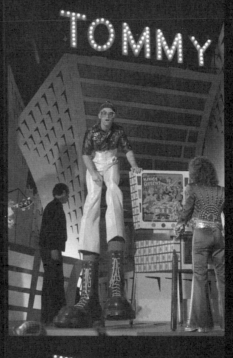
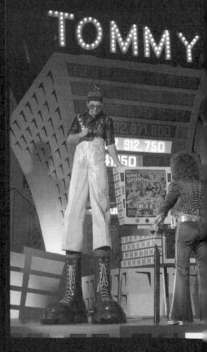
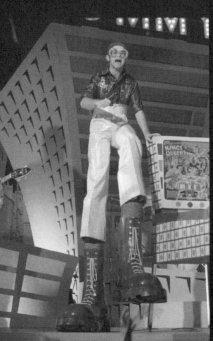
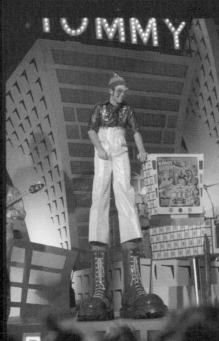
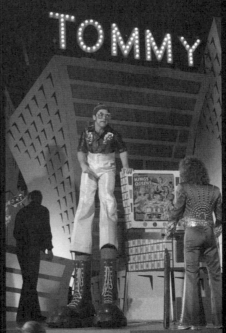
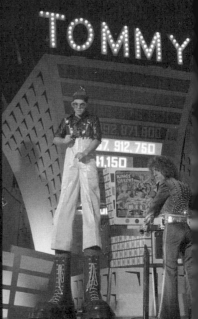

One of his most famous and well-documented concerts of all time came at the end of that triumphant tour at Madison Square Garden in New York on Thanksgiving night 1974.

Having already played to sell out crowds on both coasts, Elton wanted to finish in style and asked John Lennon if he would join him on stage. He had become friendly with Lennon and recorded the Beatle's hit Lucy In The Sky With Diamonds as a tribute to him. He had also sung backing vocals on John Lennon's Walls and Bridges album, including the single Whatever Gets You Thru The Night.

Following the break up of the Beatles four years earlier, John Lennon had developed stage fright and hadn't sung in public for years. Yet he rashly promised Elton he would join him on stage if Whatever Gets You Thru The Night reached number one — never thinking that it would.

But it did top the charts in the US that autumn — and Lennon duly kept his promise and joined Elton on stage for a surprise guest appearance in front of the 22,000-strong audience at Madison Square Garden.

The pair sang *'Lucy in the Sky With Diamonds', 'Whatever Gets You Thru the Night'* and the 1963 Beatles hit I Saw Her Standing There.

A sad postscript to the event is that it turned out to be Lennon's final stage performance before he was murdered six years later.

Elton has described the evening as being one of the most emotional of his career. Had he known that the tour itself would come to represent the absolute high point of his career he would doubtless have been even more emotional.

For while he was to enjoy more mega-hit albums, jaw-droppingly successful tours, eye-wateringly extravagant shopping trips and an ever expanding celebrity, his personal happiness was to dip as his years of drug and alcohol addiction were about to begin.

As if Elton's schedule wasn't mad enough, he also found time to film his role as the Pinball Wizard in the Ken Russell movie Tommy, based on the rock opera album by The Who.

Released in March 1975, the film was packed with stars, including Roger Daltry, Tina Turner, Jack Nicholson and Oliver Reed. Yet Elton stole the show as the cocky pinball champion of the world, the Pinball Wizard, singing Pete Townshend's song of the same name.

The shot of Elton decked out in 5ft high Doc Marten boots is an enduring image.

Elton was reportedly persuaded to take the part, which he initially refused, by a promise that he could keep the boots afterwards. They included metal calipers and leather straps to keep them in position on his legs. Balancing on them was a precarious manoeuvre, yet he belted out his number with gusto and expression.

But hardworking though he was, even Elton wasn't actually superhuman and his ridiculously tough schedule caught up with him after Caribou. His drinking had caused him to put on weight and he was in desperate need of a break. He took a trip to a tennis ranch in Arizona.

Tennis was a huge passion of his and champion player Billie Jean King was now numbered among Elton's celebrity friends. He particularly admired Billie Jean's determination and success. In honour of her King's World Tennis League team, the Philadelphia Freedoms, he recorded the up-tempo Philadelphia Freedom as his first single of 1975. It topped the charts in the US where the mid-70s Philly-sound was strong, but failed to make the top 10 in the UK,

Contact sheet of Elton john in the rock-opera movie Tommy perfoms Pinball Wizard.

where fans were perhaps not quite ready for the change of direction. Philadelphia Freedom was also the last track on his next album, the 1975 Captain Fantastic and the Brown Dirt Cowboy.

This was a loosely autobiographical album in which Bernie's lyrics ruminated on the early days when he and Elton were beginning their rise to fame as struggling songwriters in London.

It was the first album ever to enter the charts at number one in America, where it remained at the top of the charts for seven weeks.

Someone Saved my Life Tonight was another hit from this album — believed to be based on the end of his relationship with Linda Woodrow and the incident with the gas oven in London in 1969.

Elton is of course Captain Fantastic, with Bernie as the Cowboy, fixated as he always was with the American Wild West.

This album is also notable as being the last to include the original Elton John Band. Inexplicably, and latterly describing the incident as regrettable, Elton dispensed with the services of stalwarts Nigel Olsson and Dee Murray, who had contributed hugely to his success at that point. Everybody was shocked.

Guitarist Davey Johnstone and virtuoso percussionist Ray Cooper were retained, Caleb Quaye and Roger Pope were in, along with new bassist Kenny Passarelli.

In June 1975, Elton's new line up made its debut at Wembley Stadium in London watched by 75,000 fans. But it wasn't his finest

• • • • ————————————————————————▶

Elton John leaps in the air during a rehearsal at Wembley Stadium, London, June 1975

hour. Following a rollicking set from The Beach Boys who had got the crowd going, Elton and his new band confounded expectations by playing the new Captain Fantastic album, which nobody knew very well, in its entirety.

Although still at his creative peak, things were not so good for Elton on the personal front. This period is well documented in the 1975 Dodger Stadium documentary by Russell Harty, which followed Elton during his famous concert showcasing the 1975 Rock of the Westies album.

His relationship with John Reid was in trouble; he was drinking heavily and increasingly using drugs. As he told the Guardian newspaper's head rock and pop critic Alexis Petridis years later, *'In the past, particularly when I was on drugs, there was a monstrous side to me, but I'm not really like that. I can be like that briefly, but everyone can.'*

As the pressure on him grew, a darker side to his personality was emerging. Yet as the Harty documentary shows, his generosity of cash and spirit was still there. The film shows touching scenes of Elton greeting his mother and stepfather, his grandmother and other family members, together with neighbours, friends and his office staff as they arrived in Los Angeles on a plane chartered especially for them to come and see Elton perform at the mammoth Dodger Stadium baseball park, in front of a 55,000 strong crowd packed with celebrities.

The afternoon concerts took place in a highly charged, carnival atmosphere. The event was off the charts. When he was on stage his performance was as strong as ever and his fans would not have had a clue what was going on behind the showman persona. Another strong image from this time is of Elton in his sparkling baseball outfit and cap, miming a batting action for the crowd.

Ironically, just as the pressures of stardom were beginning to take a

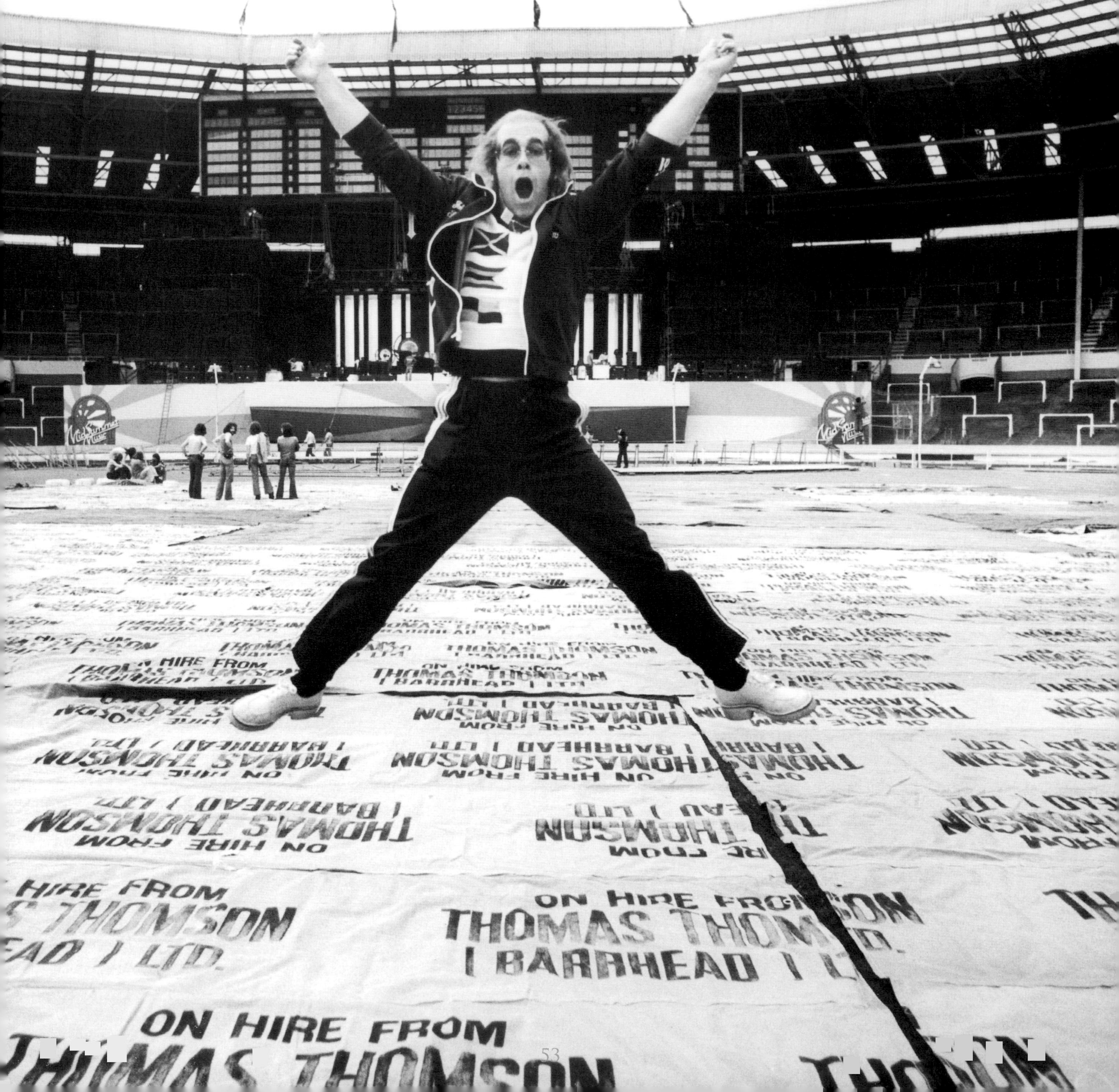
ON HIRE FROM
THOMAS THOMSON
I BARRHEAD I LTD.

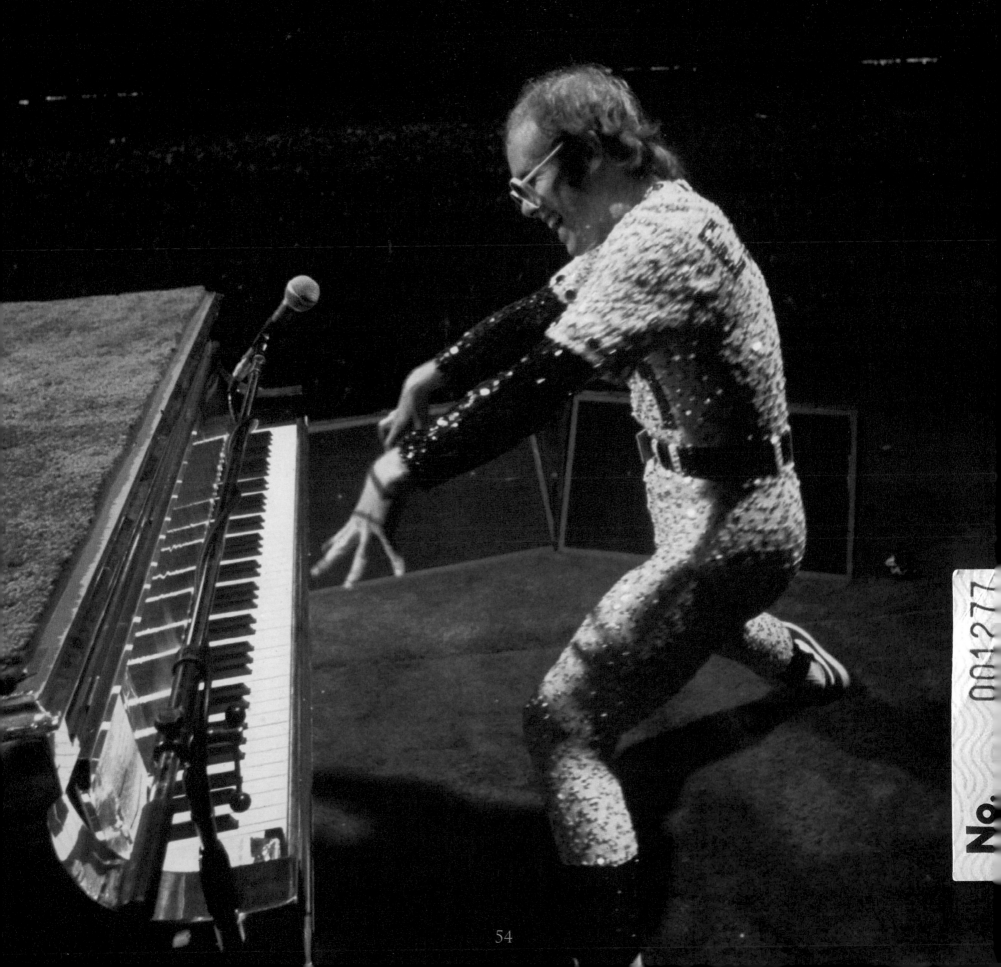

serious toll on him, Los Angeles had declared it was Elton Week and awarded him a star on the Hollywood Walk of Fame.

Yet apparently, just a few days before the shows he had taken an overdose of tranquillisers and jumped into a swimming pool in his LA mansion shouting that he was going to *'end it all'*.

Obviously he didn't. But the film shows how distressed his mother was about the change in him. She's seen crying, which at the time viewers assumed was with pride at the sight of Elton in full flow at the concert. But she later recalled how she was actually upset about the state she knew he was in.

Speaking in the Tantrums and Tiaras documentary about Elton made in 1996 she said; *'It was a terrible, terrible time, those days. It's an awful thing to see someone you love unhappy. I couldn't get near him at all. It was a different lifestyle and he'd got in with a different crowd of people.*

'There were drugs, which he denied, but I'm not daft. I knew he was taking drugs, but what can you do? I didn't see him all week until

backstage before he went on and I remember his hands were just split from playing the piano so hard and he was putting this stuff onto his skin. He looked terrible. I thought he was going to die...... I was so worried. And that was only the start of it.'

By now Elton was 28 and it is hard to overstate his fame and status at that time. Between 1972 and 1975 he had made number one in America with seven consecutive albums — a feat never accomplished before. And as well as being the most commercially successful period, these years are also held in the most regard critically.

He had public and critical acclaim, great personal wealth, luxury homes, cars, clothes and possessions beyond his wildest childhood dreams — even a yacht called Madness, permanently crewed for his annual outing. Sheila and Fred were well looked after too, wanting for nothing, wearing diamonds and gold he had given them and living in a new house.

Yet all was not well. Elton was troubled and heading in a disturbing direction...

Elton John performs in a sequinned baseball outfit at Dodger Stadium, Los Angeles, 1975; &: Ticket stub from gig

GETTING MORE MAD AND MORE ABSURD

By 1976, at the height of his heyday in America, Elton was beginning to feel the strain and pressure of half a decade of non-stop touring and recording. The lifestyle was wearing him down and he was tired and homesick.

The year had begun well enough with Elton selling up his home in Virginia Water and moving to Woodside, a large detached red brick house set in 37 acres on the edge of Windsor Great Park in Berkshire. Including a private cinema, swimming pool, stables, squash courts and a library, it was a property most befitting for a pop star of his standing.

Somewhere along the way things had gone wrong between him and John Reid and they concluded their domestic relationship — apparently by mutual consent. Things were evidently amicable enough that Reid continued to manage Elton and retained his position with The Rocket Record Company.

So Elton made the move to Windsor as a single man, but with a retinue of staff including a personal assistant, housekeeper and driver.

His decision to reside in the UK was a patriotic move; he could easily have chosen to live abroad rather than pay the UK's highest income tax rate of 83 per cent. His financial affairs were also complicated by the fact that, because he wasn't a US resident, the American Internal Revenue Service had frozen receipts from his concerts since 1973 until he had informed them of his intended permanent residency.

But Elton was keen to get home and undertook the first leg of his 'Louder than Concorde' tour to support the Rock of the Westies album in the UK during the spring of 1976. Things were smaller scale in Britain. Even a sparkling star of his stature was playing

venues unlikely to get a look in during a major music tour these days, including The Gaumont in Southampton which seated 2,229 fans, The Leeds Grand Theatre, which seated 1,500 fans, and even the Odeon in Taunton, Somerset.

But the smaller, slightly less pressured shows and lighter travel schedule suited him. It meant he was able to enjoy some home comforts and catch up with his family, especially his mother and stepfather.

The tour attracted great crowds and acclaim. The fact that part of the proceeds went towards raising funds for British athletes went down well with the public too.

Things were also going great guns at his Rocket Record Company. Since he set it up in 1972, one of the label's biggest success stories had involved the singer Kiki Dee. Kiki had been well regarded in the music business for years, but as yet had never really broken through to achieve public acclaim and hit singles. She had been the first female British singer to be signed by Tamla Motown and by the age of 26, like Elton — with whom she shares a birth month and year — was something of a veteran performer, in high demand as a background singer.

Nevertheless, it was only after she signed with Elton's label in 1973 that things started to happen for her in the charts in her own right.

The beautiful ballad 'Amoureuse' from her album Loving and Free produced by Elton had provided her first solo hit in September 1973 — the lyrics of which were written by Gary Osborne who would go on to write with Elton in the 1980s. She was also known for 'I've Got

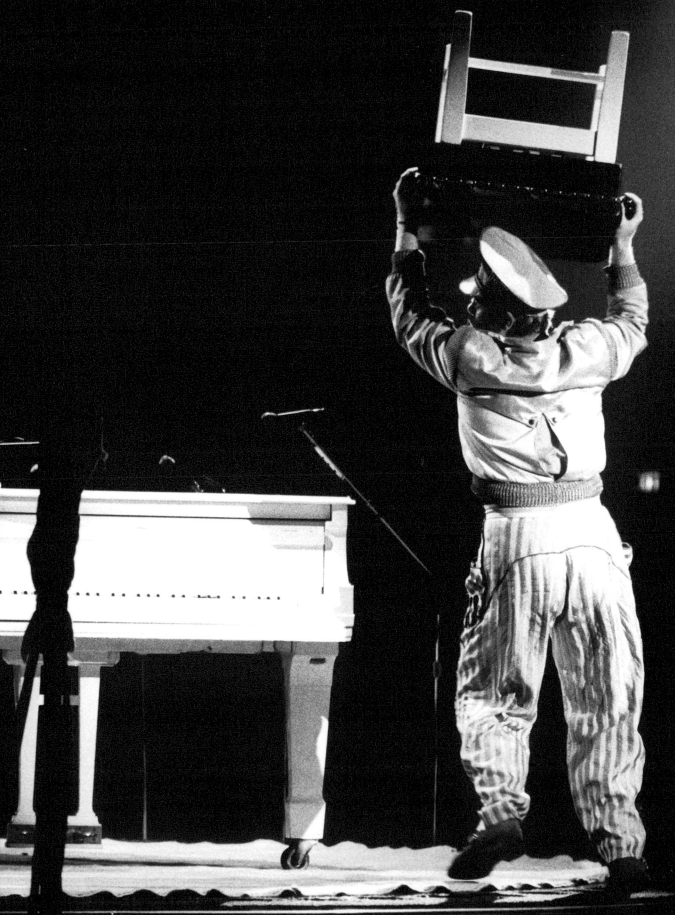

The Music In Me' which made the Top 20 in the UK and America a year later.

Elton rated her highly and featured her on backing vocals on many of his albums, including Goodbye Yellow Brick Road and Rock of the Westies. They got on well and she was Elton's first choice to duet with him on a number originally intended for Dusty Springfield who had to pull out with illness.

The song was 'Don't Go Breaking My Heart' which gave both artists their first number one in the UK (and Kiki's first in the US). At last Elton had that elusive British number one single, which topped the charts for six weeks in the summer of 1976.

Produced again by Gus Dudgeon, the song provided the soundtrack to a sunny summer, which has gone down in UK history for its record-breaking heat wave.

Despite its huge success, Don't Go Breaking My Heart had to make do with being the second-biggest selling record in 1976. Ironically, considering Elton's previous history with the competition, that year's Eurovision Song Contest had been won earlier in the year by the UK with Save Your Kisses For Me by Brotherhood of Man and that song beat Elton and Kiki in sales that year.

Strangely something similar happened in America where, although providing Elton with his sixth number one, it was the second-best-selling record after Silly Love Songs by Paul McCartney and Wings.

But none of that takes away from the success of the song which was a massive hit, topping the charts all over the world, including in Europe, Australia and Canada. Elton and Bernie had written the song using the pseudonyms Ann Orson and Carte Blanche. They

went on to win a 1976 Ivor Novello Award (given for song writing and composition) for Best Song Musically and Lyrically. In the US the Recording Industry Association of America certified the song as platinum.

Unlike most of Elton's 1970's singles, it wasn't included on an original album, although it has since appeared on greatest hits albums and as a bonus track on the re-mastered CD for Rock of the Westies in the UK.

It was actually recorded while Elton was in Toronto working on his 11th studio album, Blue Moves. So in a mirroring of the way Elton worked with Bernie, the singers weren't in the same room when it was recorded. Elton sent his vocals over from Canada to London for Kiki to drop in her lines.

Speaking to Jon Kutner and Spencer Leigh for their book 1000 UK Number One Hits, Kiki recalled that Elton had let her know which lines on the tape were hers by singing them in a high-pitched voice; 'which was quite funny. Both Elton and I were big fans of those duets on Motown by the likes of Marvin Gaye and Tammi Terrell and as there hadn't been any around for a bit, we thought we'd do one ourselves.'

Earlier that year, in May, Elton had fulfilled his final contractual obligation to Dick James' DJM Records with the release of the Here and There live album. It included two 1974 recordings, one made at the Royal Festival Hall in London and the other at the Madison Square Garden's concert in New York — though without the John Lennon songs. It is essentially a 'greatest hits' compilation covering his peak period and including earlier tracks such as Skyline Pigeon and Take Me To the Pilot bookending newer blockbuster hits including Rocket Man and Crocodile Rock.

So, at the peak of his commercial powers, Elton was free to release his next album Blue Moves in October 1976 as his first recording on his own label The Rocket Record Company. Like Goodbye Yellow Brick Road, it was a double album, but unlike that magnum opus, Blue Moves had a deliberately rather darker tone.

Elton describes this album as one of his favourites — but critics and fans at the time were not so keen, some finding fault with the fact that its 18 songs were in too many differing styles and moods. Certainly Elton was experimenting with alternative sub-genres and a mix of musicians at the time. Its best-known track is Sorry Seems To Be The Hardest Word which was released as a single.

'The interesting thing about Sorry Seems To Be The Hardest Word is that it's one of the rare occasions when Elton played me a melody line that inspired a lyric, as opposed to our routine of the lyrics always coming first,' Bernie explains on his website. "He was messing around on the piano one day and was playing something and asked me what did I think. It was actually pretty immediate, the title and the first couple of lines came into my head in a way that I guess I felt they were already there and just needed a little prompting.

'It's a pretty simple idea, but one that I think everyone can relate to at one point or another in their life. That whole idealistic feeling people get when they want to save something from dying when they basically know deep down inside that it's already dead. It's that heartbreaking, sickening part of love that you wouldn't wish on anyone if you didn't know that it's inevitable that they're going to experience it one day.'

That hit aside, there were some negative reviews for the album as a whole. According to Rolling Stone magazine at the time the album contained; '....nowhere near enough good songs to justify

the extended length. The Village Voice, rated the album as just a 'C' describing it as 'impossibly weepy' and 'excessive'. Retrospectively, Lindsay Planer of Allmusic wrote that; 'The immense creativity that had spurred Elton John to realise no less than 11 studio albums in under seven years was beginning to show signs of inevitable fatigue'.

But nevertheless, the album did make number three in both the British and American charts.

The second leg of the 'Louder than Concorde' landed in America at the end of June and the 29 sell out dates culminated with seven nights at Madison Square Garden in New York where Elton famously wore his famous Statue of Liberty costume. Those concerts broke the box office record for a rock act by playing to audiences of around 140,000 people.

But the punishing performance schedule was exhausting. However glamorous it sounds on the surface, a life spent in luxury hotels and private jets, loses its allure eventually.

Speaking to journalist Cliff Jahr in an interview for Rolling Stone he described his last night at Madison Square Garden, as '..... a pretty weird night, a very sad occasion, I must say. It came to the point where I sang 'Yellow Brick Road' and I thought, "I don't have to sing this anymore", and it made me quite happy inside.'

Seemingly almost thinking aloud he continued .... 'Yeah, it could be the last gig forever. I'm definitely not retiring but I want to put my energies elsewhere for a while. ..... I always do things by instinct and I just know it's time to cool it; I mean, who wants to be a 45-year-old entertainer in Las Vegas like Elvis?'

But the most famous section of the interview eclipsed those

Elton with Davey Johnstone at Madison Square Garden during 'Louder Than Concorde' tour on August 10 1976

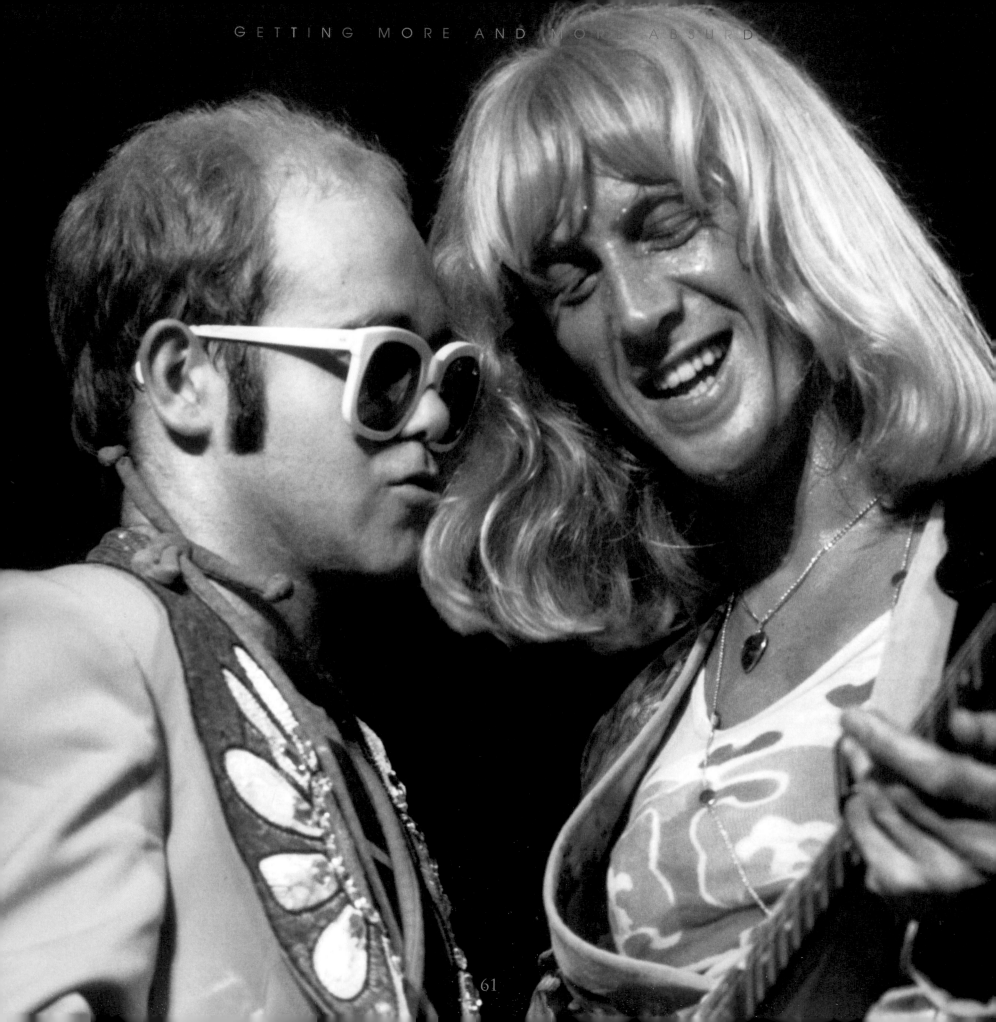

musings. Elton unexpectedly, and perhaps to shake things up a bit, announced that he was bisexual.

'My sexual life? Um, I haven't met anybody I would like to have any big scenes with. It's strange that I haven't. I know everyone should have a certain amount of sex, and I do, but that's it, and I desperately would like to have an affair. I crave to be loved. That's the part of my life I want to have come together in the next two or three years and it's partly why I'm quitting the road.

'I don't know what I want to be exactly. I'm just going through a stage where any sign of affection would be welcome on a sexual level. I'd rather fall in love with a woman eventually because I think a woman probably lasts much longer than a man. But I really don't know. I've never talked about this before. Ha, ha.'

Asked outright by Cliff Jahr if he was saying he was bisexual he replied: *'There's nothing wrong with going to bed with somebody of your own sex. I think everybody's bisexual to a certain degree. I don't think it's just me. It's not a bad thing to be. I think you're bisexual. I think everybody is.'*

Cliff replied that; 'A lot of readers will go, wow,' to which Elton replied; 'Well, I don't think so, there shouldn't be too much reaction, but you probably know those things better than me. Nobody's had the balls to ask me about it before. I would have said something all along if someone had asked me, but I'm not going to come out and say something just to be – I do think my personal life should be personal.'

Although Elton's sexuality was basically an open secret within the industry, such a public announcement did of course generate mass coverage in the mainstream press and on TV channels.

America has always been a more conservative country than the UK and the American press coverage at the time suggested that the public was stunned by the news — perhaps having believed there was truth in the jaunty lyrics of Don't Go Breaking My Heart that Elton had sung with Kiki Dee. Certainly his manager John Reid, who had not been consulted about the interview, had been against such an announcement. It was a very different time and those around Elton were concerned about the effect of such an interview on record sales.

However, when Sorry Seems To Be The Hardest Word came out as a single a few weeks after the interview it still made the American top 10 and reached number 11 in the UK.

Although Elton was not **to return to the** subject of his **sexuality for several** years, he was **true to his word about** taking **time out.**

But on his return to England Elton found that musical tastes were changing. Bands were overtaking solo performers in popularity and punk rock was taking a strong hold. In just a year's time the Clash would announce their proposed changing of the musical guard with their single, 1977 including the lyric 'No Elvis, Beatles or the Rolling Stones in 1977', picking up on the public mood among the new generation of record buyers who were tiring of rock superstars.

With the UK economy in recession, young people were looking for new musical heroes who were more like them. They couldn't relate to the lifestyle and riches of rock superstars, but were more easily able to connect with the new rebellious wave of punk. The Sex Pistols' lead singer Johnny Rotten also spoke disparagingly about mega-stars like Elton who he lumped in with the *'Establishment'* which punk railed against.

• • • • ————————————————➤

Elton John joins Kiki Dee for the song 'Don't Go Breaking My Heart' onstage in Central Park on August 2, 1977

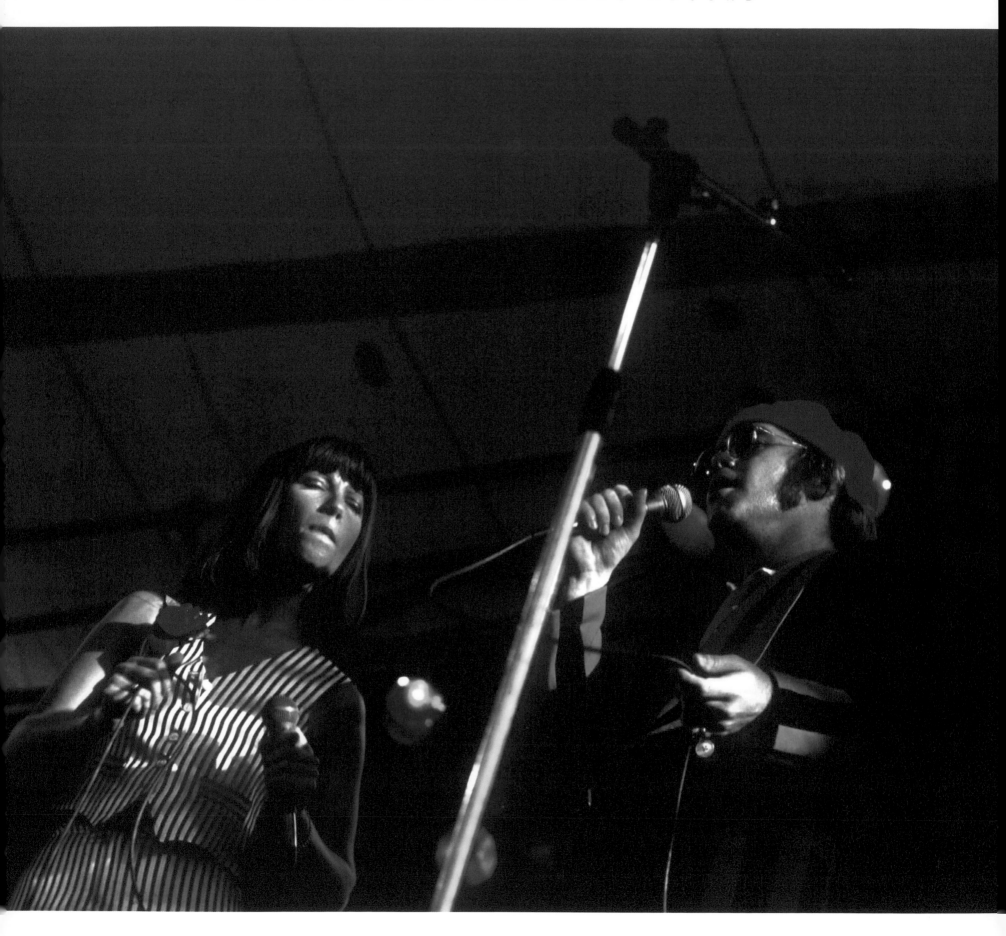

Worn out and slightly bored, Elton, now aged 30, slipped briefly under the public radar, gave no interviews, made no records and didn't perform, save for a couple of charity events. In true diva fashion, while headlining a gala charity concert at Wembley Arena in November 1977, he announced that that night's performance would be his last show.

Looking back on that time during a live television interview in America with Phil Donahue in 1980, Elton said; 'I was basically unhappy with my whole life; the situation in my personal life…….. By 1976 I had had enough….. It was just music, music, music, but then it got to the stage where there were more important things and I became very unhappy and I had to stop   I'd say listen, you're going to go crazy or you're going to go straight down the tubes, so I stopped.

'The discipline was slipping, and so was I. I don't like spending a long time in a recording studio. You get lazy. The more successful you are you the more lax you get and you get sloppy….. and you can't afford to get sloppy if you are playing in front of people who have paid to see you, or you are making records that people are spending good money to buy.

'Your personal attitude reflects on your professional attitude and my personal attitude definitely wasn't very good.'

Laying off from work for a while meant Elton was then free to turn his attentions to his home, his record company and his beloved Watford Football Club. Football was one of the things he missed most about the UK.

Since standing on the terraces, with his father Stan back in the early 1950s, Elton had remained a huge fan of Watford. With his interest in touring waning, but his appetite for work undiminished, he needed a new challenge.

So he took up an offer to become club chairman of the club and vowed to improve the team's fortunes by taking them from their position in the lowly Fourth Division to the top of the game.

He also tried to relax, played a lot of tennis which he loves, and travelled. During his musical hiatus he also had time to start tackling his on-going hair loss by undergoing a hair transplant operation and was hopeful of a good result.

But without the discipline of work he had no need or inclination to curb his appetite for drink and drugs, which in turn led to a period of sexual promiscuity. Looking back over that time Elton has described feeling very lucky that he didn't contract AIDS.

The substance abuse also made him difficult to work and live with. Despite his entourage he was lonely. Even Sheila fell out with him in a row over housekeeping.

Drugs and drink have always been easily available around the music scene and for someone like Elton with an addictive personality and prone to excess it was inevitable that once ensnared he would struggle.

At first he could handle it — the cocaine may even have helped stoke the unfathomable physical stamina he showed in maintaining the relentless pace of the headily successful years between 1970-76. While small amounts of cocaine often improve confidence and energy, large amounts of the drug causes agitation and restlessness and can lead to erratic and risky behaviour. And that's just before severe medical complications, such as heart problems, seizures and strokes. So of course it came to affect him badly.

Elton would only perform three times in 1978 and the next few years were fallow times in the charts. Bernie had his problems as well. His

Elton John dressed all in black with black heeled boots on a long driveway, 1978

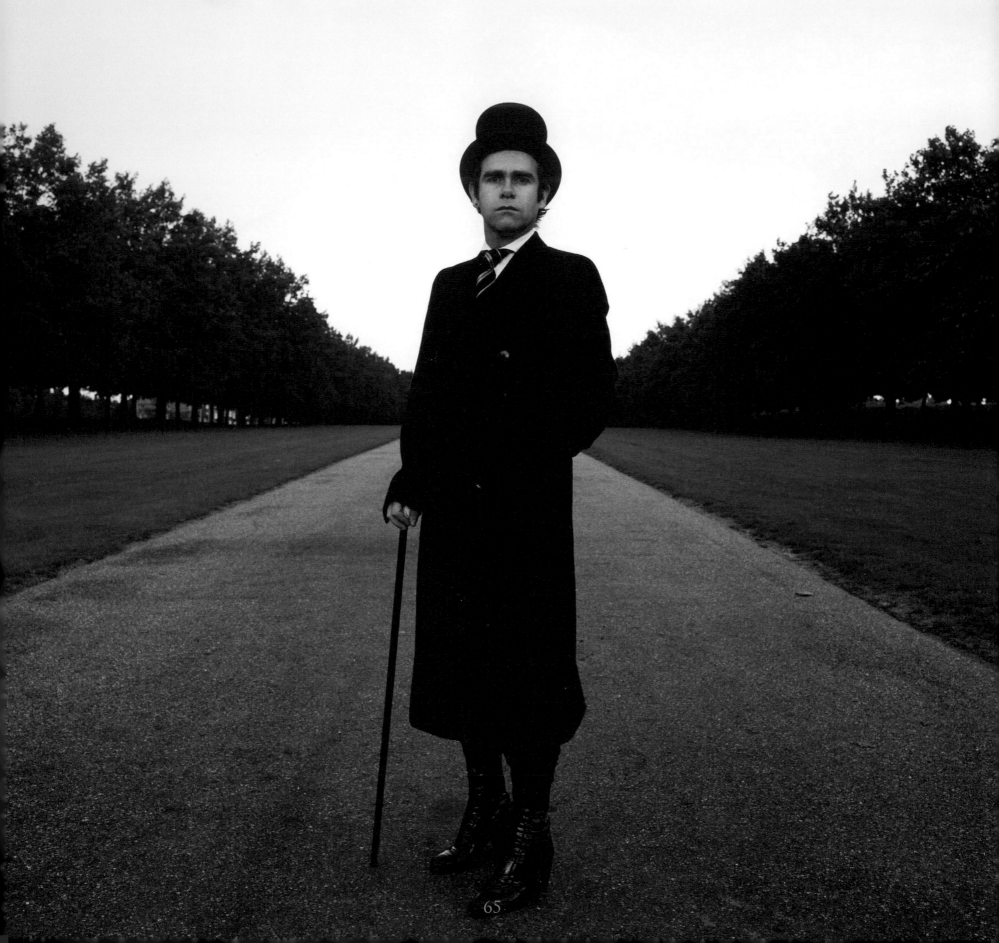

marriage to Maxine had ended and he was back in America battling alcohol addition. The pair never fell out, but went their separate ways for a while.

Gus Dudgeon was another professional casualty of Elton's life around this time. Having become disenchanted with his role as a director at the Rocket Record Company, Gus tried to strengthen his hand by threatening to leave if no one listened to his opinion. Nobody tried to dissuade him — so he left, selling his shares to John Reid. He continued to work successfully in the business with many and varied artists such as Elkie Brooks and Chris Rea.

But despite seeming not to care about the music business, Elton was still devoted to Watford and tried never to miss a game, home or away. One of his first acts as chairman had been to bring in a new club manager, Graham Taylor who quickly brought the club the sort of success that life-long supporters such as Elton had only dreamed they would see.

In Taylor's first season in charge (1977-78) Watford won promotion to the Third Division — a feat Elton described as being 'better than having a record at number one'.

Elton meant business and was happy to splash his cash on buying new players. A combination of his money and Graham Taylor's management flair propelled the team through the next season (1978-79) at the end of which they went up into the Second Division. Things were getting better and better at Watford.

Around that time it seemed Elton regained some of his musical mojo as well.

He became interested in a new producer, Thom Bell, and felt able to get back into the studio — though he was disappointed with the work they did together in the end.

A video for Ego — a stand-alone single left over from the Blue Moves sessions, released in 1978 -shows a leaner-looking Elton in a toned-down costume of fedora and suit and tie. This song — and Elton's look — shows him during a period of transition, reflecting on the life of rock star whose fame went to his head.

When Elton was ready to work on another album — his first for two years — he employed a new lyricist, Gary Osborne, of Amoureuse fame.

The resulting album was 'A Single Man' which included two Top 20 singles in the UK, though not in America. These were Part-Time Love and Song for Guy — which got as high as number 5 and was named as a tribute to Guy Burchett, a young Rocket messenger who had been killed in a motorcycle accident.

This album is notable as the first example of Elton singing in a lower register. He had also produced the album himself, in the absence of Gus Dudgeon.

Rolling Stone — his confessional magazine of choice in America, didn't review it well. It described the album's 'move toward simplicity' as 'a step into emptiness, …… nothing more than a collection of trivial hooks performed about as perfunctorily as possible'.

But as usual a bad review wasn't going to stop the Elton machine. His fans liked it and the album went gold in the UK and Europe and platinum in America and Canada.

Although he was still in the grip of substance abuse and its related

Live onstage at Drury Lane Theatre, 1979

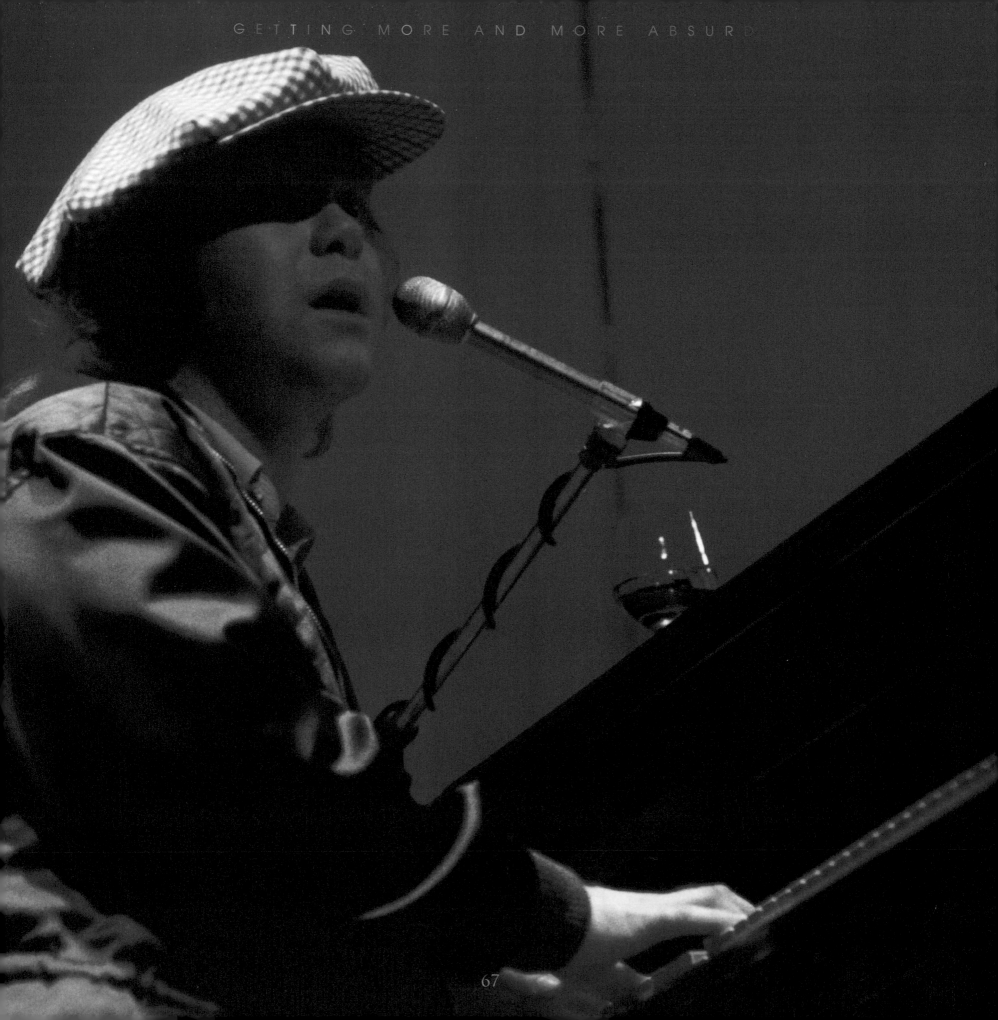

health complications, the lure of life on the road was enough for Elton to ignore medical advice and start playing live again in 1979.

He said it would be different, using smaller venues and dispensing with the theatrical fireworks…until he got the opportunity to become the first Western rock star to play in the Soviet Union.

Continuing to break new ground, in May 1979, and accompanied by percussionist Ray Cooper, Elton included the dates in the then still communist country, as part of his European tour to support the A Single Man album.

'We decided to try and play places that we had never sort of played before,' he told United Press International. 'Usually, most rock 'n' roll people go to places where they can make money, but I've had enough of doing that. I want to see different people all over the world.' Elton played four concerts in Leningrad (now St. Petersburg) followed by four more in Moscow. Each night featured a solo set from Elton on a single grand Steinway piano and an electric CP80 -- followed by a second set with percussionist Ray Cooper accompanying on drums.

He was criticised for going there because relations were strained between Russia and the West — but says he wouldn't have missed it for the world. He took just a dozen people with him, including his mother and stepfather.

The concerts in Russia were a success and in fact the whole tour was a sellout as fans welcomed Elton back. A Single Man went to number 8 in the UK and number 25 in America, winning gold and platinum discs respectively.

Encouraged by this success Elton made a more disco-influenced album, 'Victim of Love'.

Disco was big in the late 1970s culture — best exemplified by the success of the Saturday Night Fever movie and its Bee Gees soundtrack. But Elton's experimental take on the genre was generally poorly received.

Comprising just seven tracks and coming in at only 35 minutes long, this album is Elton's shortest and the only one on which he doesn't play piano. He didn't seem to have the heart to promote it and in the end the recording only made it to number 35 in the American charts and number 41 in the UK. Nothing much has been heard of it since.

Elton's final album release of the 1970s was 21 at 33 — so named because he was 33 and this was his 21st album, counting the double albums Goodbye Yellow Brick Road and Blue Moves as two recordings each. It included collaborations with Tom Robinson and Judy Tzuke, and did produce a hit single, the ballad Little Jeannie written with Gary Osborne.

This was better received than his previous offering and saw him restored to the top in the charts, making number two in the UK and number 13 in the US.

While recording 21 at 33, he also laid down most of the tracks for his the 1981 release The Fox — his first for Geffen Records in the US. Elton had moved to David Geffen's label after negotiations to extend his agreement with MCA broke down.

Although the album was critically acclaimed in the UK and made number 12 in the charts, it fared less well in America. With sales of only 300,000, the album received little airplay and generated no hit singles.

But his commercial fortunes were to return in the early 1980s. Elton reassembled the old Elton John Band lineup with Nigel Olsson and

Elton John at the Rosemont Horizon in Rosemont, Illinois, September 6, 1980

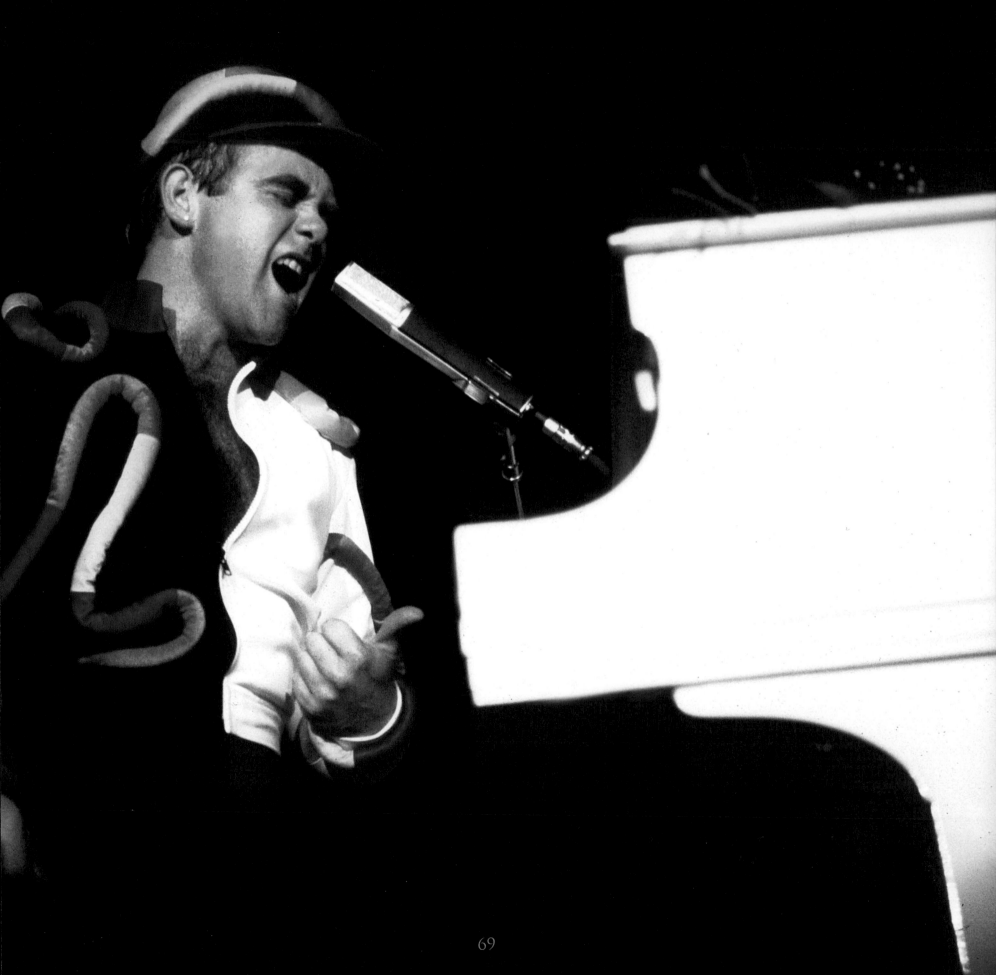

Dee Murray back in and Bernie, after a successful stint in rehab and a new girlfriend, was ready to resume their partnership.

They wrote together again for Elton's 16th studio album Jump Up! which includes the hit Blue Eyes and the tribute to John Lennon Empty Garden (Hey Hey Johnny).

This album was written mainly with Bernie, but also includes a few tracks on which Elton collaborated with Gary Osborne and Tim Rice. He had known Tim since the early 1970s when both men were working in London's record industry.

In 1983, after deciding that he wanted to return to working with Bernie full time, Elton made a chart comeback with the well-received album Too Low for Zero and its two big hit singles I'm Still Standing and I Guess That's Why They Call It The Blues.

Elton was back to working at a frenetic pace. Despite his continued heavy drinking and partying he was indeed *still standing'*. Issuing an up-tempo single of that name worked brilliantly as a metaphor for his own resilience, although Bernie's lyrics actually discuss moving on following a break up.

Although Elton famously hated filming, the video he made for this single is probably his best. Shot on the Cote d'Azur, Elton is dressed like a true song and dance man complete with hat and cane, and performs amid a crowd of scantily dressed dancers in a tightly choreographed affair. It was perfect timing for the early days of MTV, which had launched in 1981, and gave him a top five hit in the UK, a number one in Canada and made number 12 in the states. The album itself spent a year on the Billboard chart.

The follow up to this album was Breaking Hearts in June 1984 which

made number two in the UK charts and achieved platinum in the US at number 20. It also spawned the hit singles Passengers and Sad Songs (Say So Much).

The **album** is also notable for being **the** last to feature **all four** core members of the classic 'Elton **John Band'** lineup **playing** together.

Despite being back on form in the music business, Elton was far from being back to normal personally. He was partying too hard and suffering too much. As the drink and drugs still had a hold he also became bulimic. Given the shape he was in it was amazing that he could still work. But it was not easy to be around him, professionally or personally, as he was moody and demanding — searching for personal happiness.

But he then shocked everyone by appearing to find the soul mate he'd always wanted — but in the shape of a woman. She was his close friend and sound engineer Renate Blauel. After a whirlwind romance they married on Valentine's Day 1984 in Australia where Elton was on tour.

Many suspected the marriage as being set up to cover the fact that Elton was gay — and he has subsequently hinted that he was embarking on a heterosexual relationship in an attempt to find the happiness he sought.

Always on the look out for a story, the British press watched developments in the marriage closely. The couple were often separated by work which led to frequent speculation about their happiness together.

• • • • ⟶

Elton John poses by a pool circa 1981

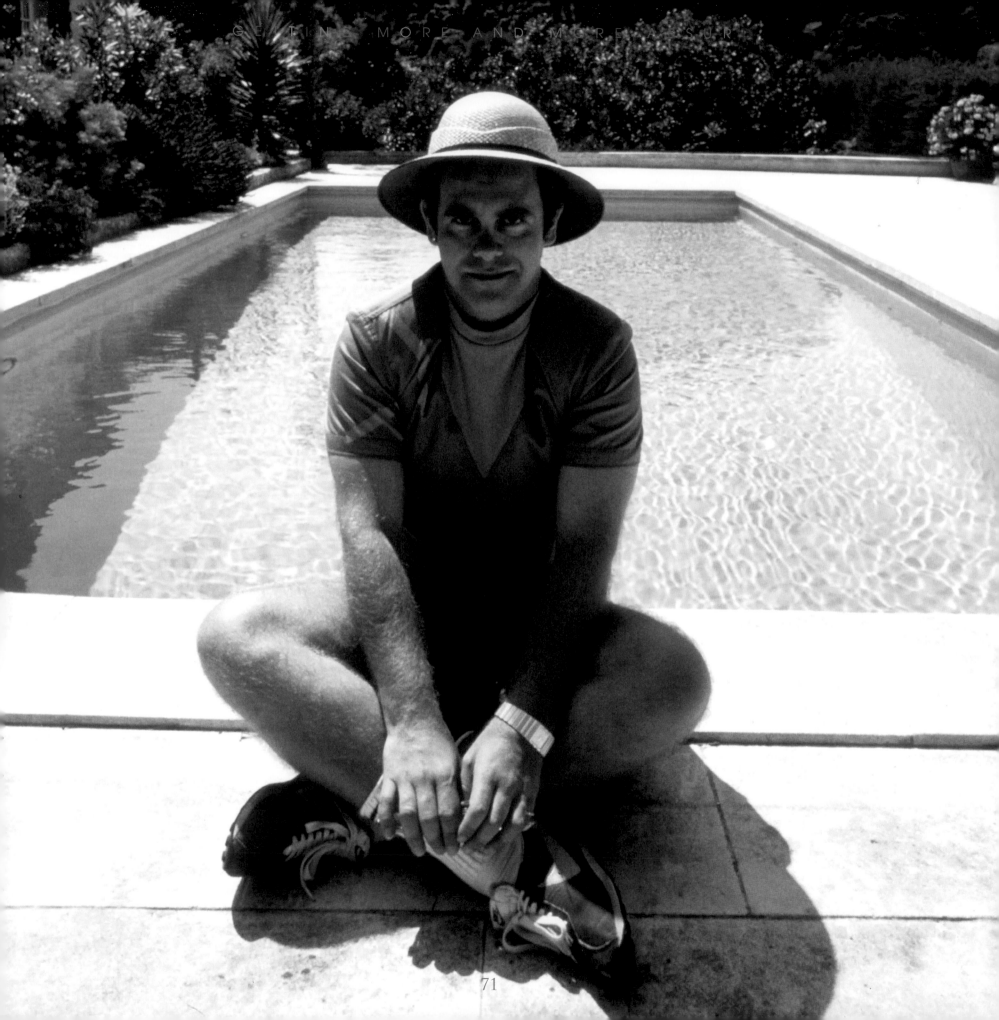

As well as being the year of his marriage, 1984 was also important for Elton because his beloved Watford football team made the FA Cup Final. Elton's had made good on his promise to propel them up the tables and the team had secured promotion to the First Division in 1982.

Although they lost their cup final to Everton 2-0, it was a great day for Elton and the culmination of years of hard work. The air of show biz glamour he had lent the team undoubtedly lifted their spirits.

He would invite the entire club staff to his Windsor home at the start of every season for a party, typically including a fun five-a-side kick-about and a Punch and Judy show for the children. And in return Elton has credited his involvement with Watford as keeping him grounded at times. It enabled him to mix with people from outside the music business and to hear the occasional home truth — including some brutally cruel taunts and chants from the fans on the terraces.

As well as playing Bob Geldof's Live Aid charity concert in July 1985, Elton was busy with another album, Ice On Fire. In another game of musical chairs, Nigel Olsson and Dee Murray were out again, while Gus Dudgeon was back in, for the first time since Blue Moves. The album made number three in the UK, but was less well received in America where it only reached 48 in the charts.

Nikita, released at the end of 1985 was the major hit from this collection of tracks. Giving Elton his biggest success with a single at home since the mid-70s, it reached number three in the UK and number seven in the US — helped by a video directed by Ken Russell.

The mid tempo ballad tells the love story of a Western tourist (depicted by Elton in the video) falling in love with an East German border guard. Tension was high between the West and the Soviet-controlled East up until the 1990s — it was around the time of the Olympic boycotts so the song chimed perfectly with the mood and sentiments of the time.

The next album Leather Jackets was to be Elton's last collaboration with Gus — and sadly did not represent a high point in their body of work together. In fact it was disappointing — the poorest-charting album of his career and producing no top 40 hit singles in the UK or the US. 'I was not a well budgie' conceded Elton years afterwards.

He was indeed in a personal and creative trough; his life dominated by cocaine use and alcohol.

In various interviews after 2010 Elton has admitted to the story about a particular example of his diva-like behavior when having been up all night on cocaine, he rang his office to complain it was too windy outside his hotel room.

Montreux Pop Festival, 1984

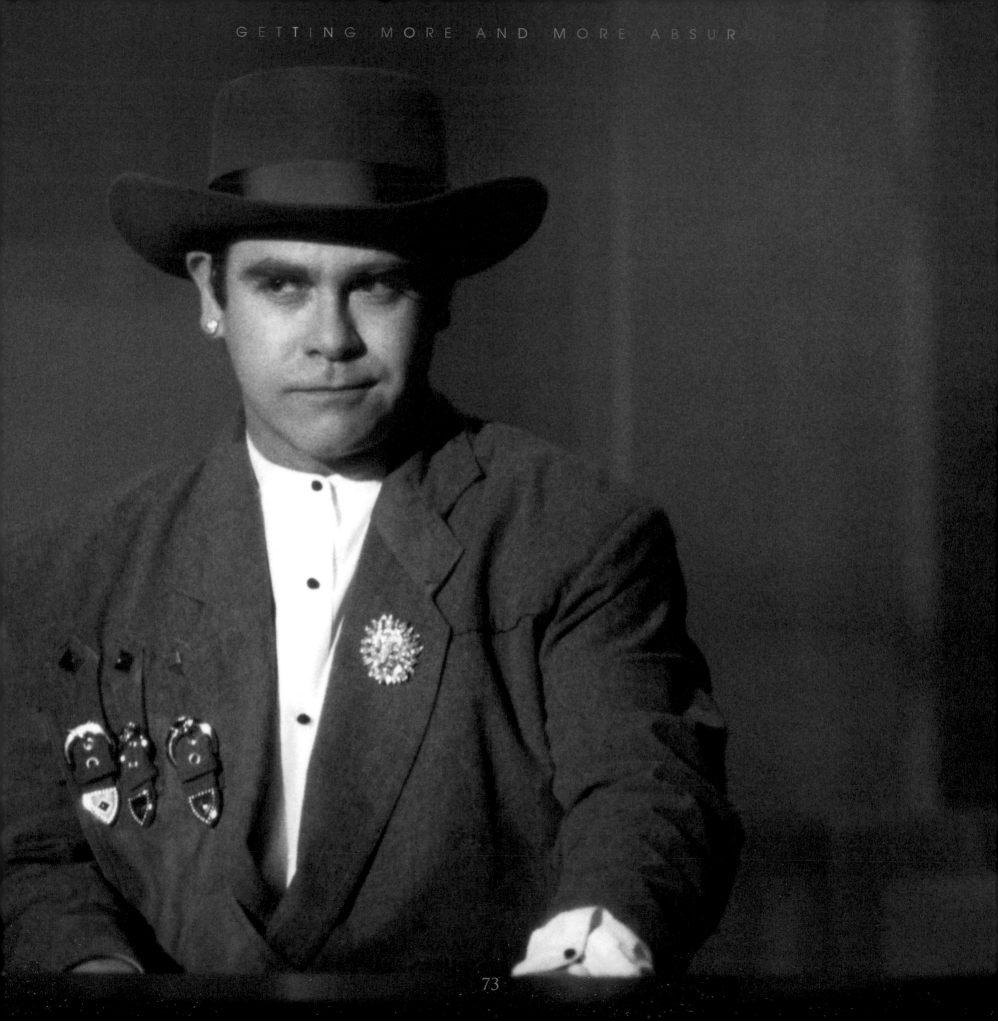

...d been up for a couple of days at the inn on the Park, as it was then, on Park Lane in London, and I was still up at 11 o'clock in the morning.

'I rang the office and spoke to a guy called Robert Key and I said, Robert, it's far too windy here, can you do something about it?'

'It wasn't a tantrum as such but as reality goes, it was pretty far off the chart. Apparently when he put the phone down, Robert said to the rest of the office — "she's finally lost it, she's finally lost the plot".'

Elton was also experiencing problems with his voice and underwent surgery to remove non-malignant growths on his vocal chords. Of course there was worry beforehand that it could be cancer — so the final diagnosis was a relief, although for a singer any surgery involves big concerns over future vocal abilities. Fortunately after rest and recovery Elton was able to sing again, although his voice was deeper and more resonant and his falsetto register was diminished.

But worse was to follow. 1987 was truly an annus horribilis. He had a huge battle with The Sun newspaper after they published false accusations about him, including that he had had sex with rent boys. Elton won his libel case against them, but it was naturally a huge strain on a man already battling his own demons and addictions. Speaking afterwards Elton said; 'It caused me great grief. But you have to make a stand. The tabloid press was just running rife over everybody and I just wouldn't put up with it. I wouldn't be bullied. All I wanted to do was clear my name'.

That wasn't Elton's only brush with the legal system in the 1980s. Having pored over Elton and Bernie's original contracts with their early mentor Dick James, John Reid had concluded that unpaid royalties were due. In a landmark case for the British music industry Elton sued Dick James, contesting that his organization had taken unfair financial advantage. The verdict was that DJM were to pay substantial backdated royalties, but the judge rejected allegations of fraud and cleared Dick James of any personal blame.

Sitting in court with Dick James, his former friend and mentor, was painful for Elton and with the case being followed swiftly by The Sun's shenanigans, his response was predictable — more drugs, drink and, of course, work.

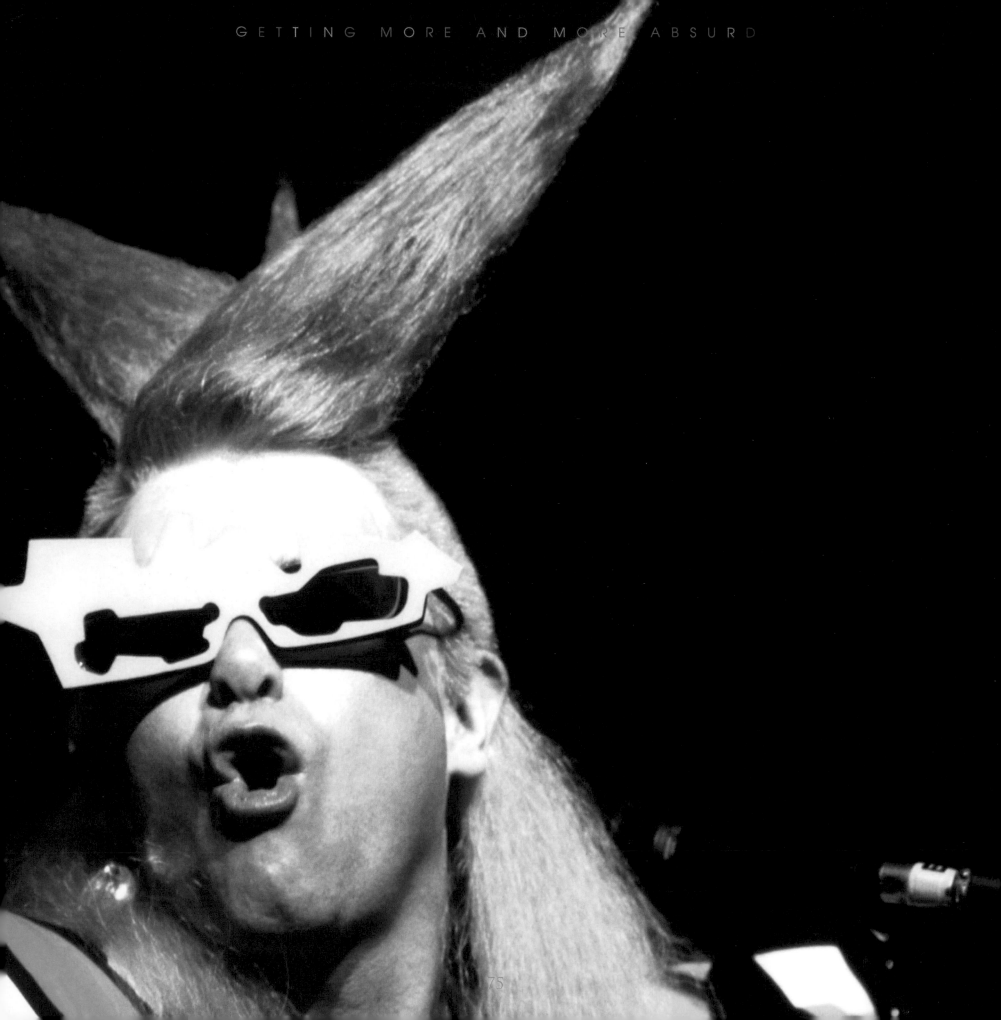

I GUESS THAT'S WHY THEY CALL IT THE BLUES

1987 - 96

The type of stress Elton was under during his marriage, including press intrusion and ongoing battles with addictions, would have strained any union — whether of convenience or otherwise. In 1988 Elton and Renate announced that they were to divorce, parting amicably *'and genuinely intend to remain best of friends.'*

In an interview with Rolling Stone later that year, Elton came out fully, saying that he *'was comfortable being gay'.*

Renate has never spoken about the marriage since and Elton has only ever referred to his ex-wife in the most glowing of terms.

When Elton was supporting a proposal to allow gay marriage in Australia in 2017, he made a rare reference to her, saying; *'Many years ago, I chose Australia for my wedding to a wonderful woman for whom I have so much love and admiration. I wanted more than anything to be a good husband, but I denied who I really was, which caused my wife sadness, and caused me huge guilt and regret.*

'To be worthy of someone's love, you have to be brave enough and clear eyed enough to be honest with yourself and your partner.'

In behaviour common to many people following a break up, Elton took the opportunity to clear out his life in other ways too — selling much of his collection of memorabilia, amounting to some 2,000 items during an historic four-day sale at Sotheby's auction house in London which raised millions of pounds.

The antiques, art and costumes he cleared out included the 5-ft high boots he wore in the movie *'Tommy'* and his *'Captain Fantastic'* pinball machine, etchings by Rembrandt and Picasso, a Magritte painting of a swimming fish draped with strings of pearls, gorgeous Lalique glass, Tiffany lamps, Bugatti furniture and a flock of Art Deco and Art Nouveau pieces a museum official said were *'good enough to kill for'.*

Some 25 of his famous stage costumes, including his Statue of Liberty number, went under the hammer, as well as 100 pairs of his stage glasses and his gold records.

'There's been so much stuff it's been like walking into a warehouse,' Elton said at the time. *'I want somewhere to sit rather than somewhere to stand.'*

Divested of his *'stuff'* Elton then threw himself full throttle back into his career. He hit the road to promote album number 21 — Reg Strikes Back — including another five sell out concerts at Madison Square Garden.

Reg Strikes Back was his first recording after a successful throat operation and named presumably to demonstrate his victory over recent adversity. The album had a cover picturing costumes from the collection he had auctioned off and represented another *'come back'* of a type. Its hit single was I Don't Wanna Go On With You Like That which reached number two in America, though it only edged into the top 30 in the UK.

He followed this up with Sleeping with the Past. He and Bernie were going great guns again and this time it was to pay off big time. The single released from the album was the double A-side Sacrifice/Healing Hands which topped the UK chart in 1990 giving Elton his long dreamed for solo number one in his homeland. The album itself went three times platinum.

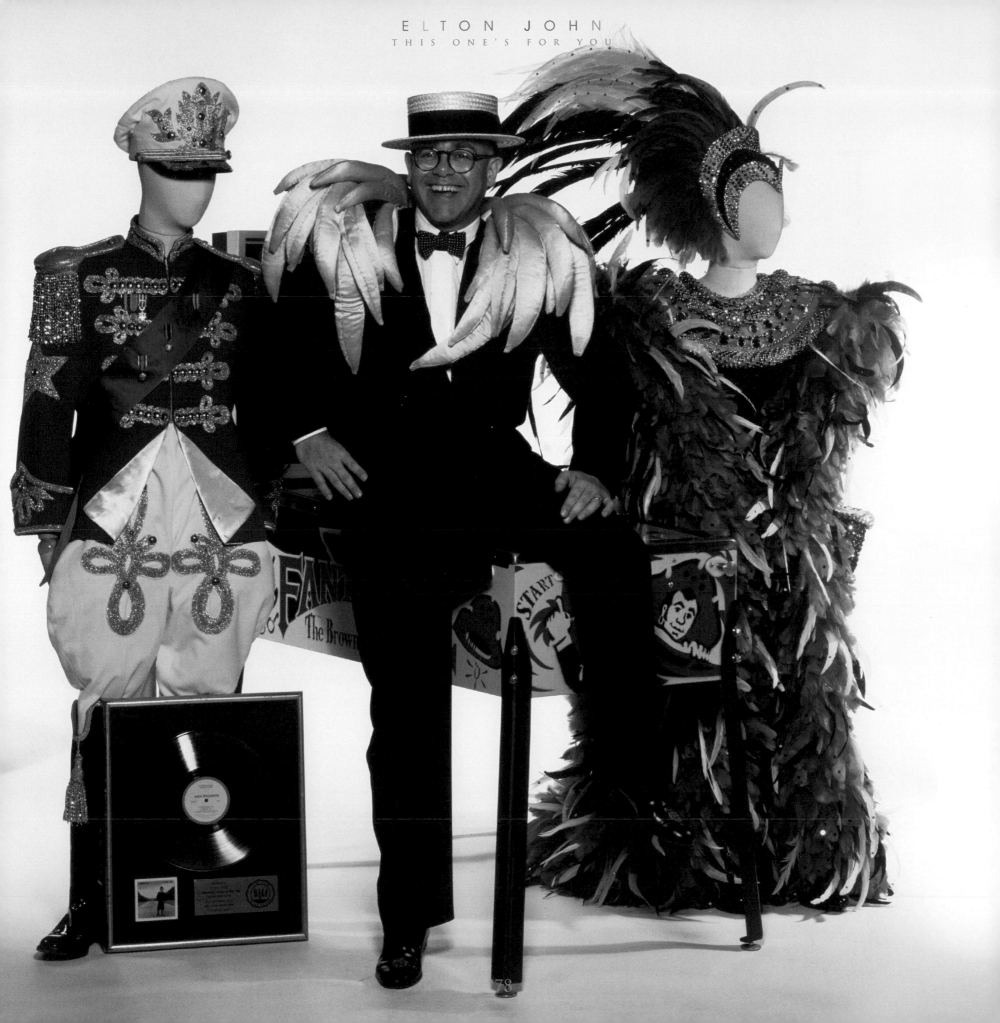

First released in 1989, Sacrifice had made little impact until British DJ Steve Wright heard it while on holiday in the states and revived it on his radio show. Bernie wrote the song as a very personal rumination about the importance of fidelity. By this time he had been through another divorce, from second wife Toni Russo, and he described the song as having an adult lyric — a million miles away from the idealism of Your Song.

The following year brought Elton another number one hit. A recording of the guest concert appearance he had made on George Michael's cover of Elton and Bernie's hit from Caribou, *'Don't Let The Sun Go Down On Me'* was released as a single and topped the charts on both sides of the Atlantic.

Renewed chart success came as Elton was reaching a personal nadir. Then two things happened to jolt him out of his despair.

The first was the death of an 18-year-old boy called Ryan White who had become HIV positive following a blood transfusion to treat his haemophilia.

HIV/AIDS was rife and misunderstood in the 1980s and early 1990s. Most commonly caught by having unprotected sex or sharing infected needles, it was at that time considered a *'gay plague'* and Elton considered himself lucky to have escaped its clutches given his lifestyle during those years.

Ryan had a terminal AIDS diagnosis at the age of 13 and used the last years of his life to campaign to remove the stigma around the disease.

Touched by his story, which gained national press attention in the

United States, Elton befriended and supported Ryan and his family — to the extent of spending the last weeks of Ryan's life at his bedside. He paid for and sang at his funeral in April 1990 and the whole experience affected him deeply, causing him to reflect upon his own life.

It was then that he decided to support research into AIDS and he donated all British royalties from Sacrifice to four AIDS charities.

Truly shaken by his association with Ryan and his family, Elton was dealt another blow when his then partner Hugh Williams checked into rehab having tired of his own addictions.

At first Elton took the news badly. Hugh's decision to clean up his act led Elton to question his own lifestyle and face some harsh truths. When he had calmed down he came to see that his own behaviour and addictions were also intolerable and decided he had to deal with his problems and sort out his life.

Answering a question from TV interviewer Piers Morgan in 2010, about how close he came to death during his dark times, Elton replied that he was *'very close. I mean, I would have an epileptic seizure and turn blue, and people would find me on the floor and put me to bed, and then 40 minutes later I'd be snorting another line [of cocaine].'*

Elton checked into rehab in Parkside Lutheran Hospital, Chicago on July 29, 1990 and set about dealing with his multiple addictions of drugs, alcohol and bulimia.

One of his tasks in therapy was to apologise to everyone his addictions had affected and to write about his history of substance abuse.

Elton John with some of the items he put up for auction at Sotheby's, London, 1988

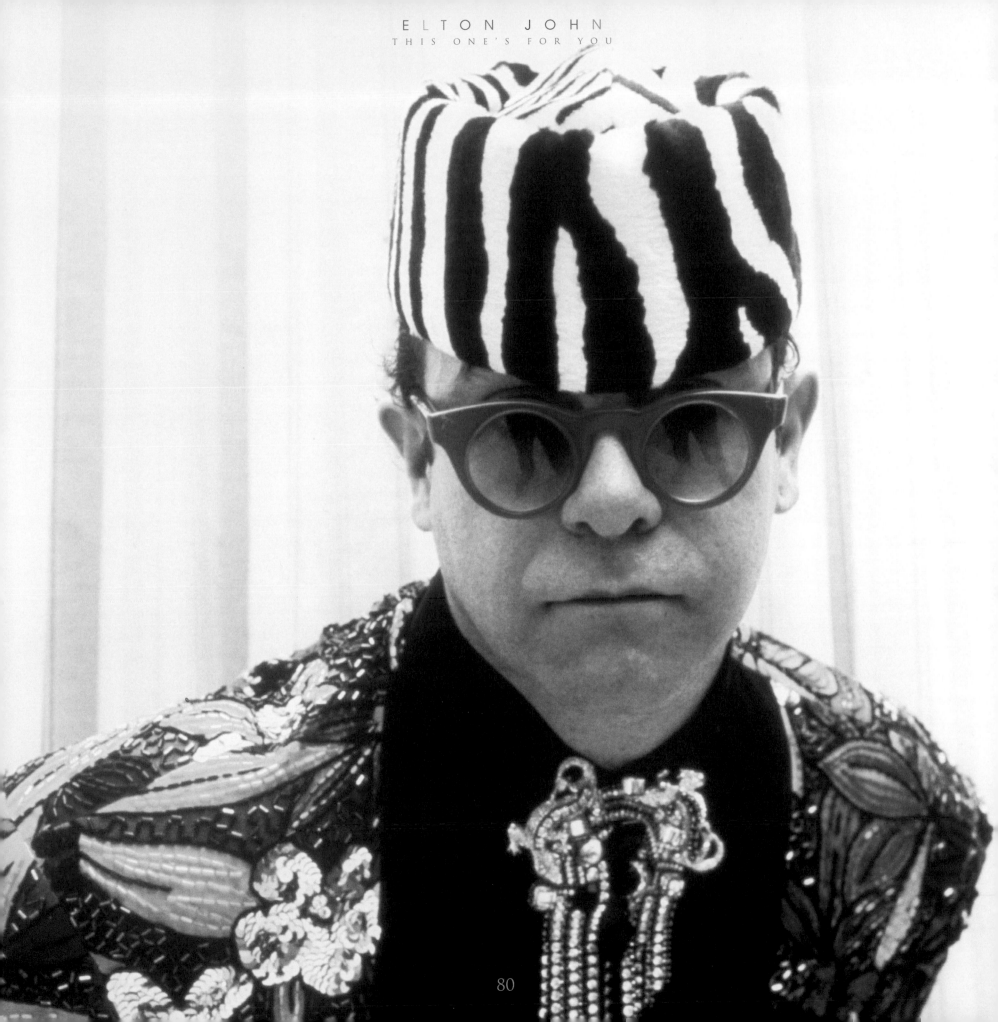

In a farewell letter to cocaine, he included the telling lines; *'I don't want you and I to have the same grave. I'm fed up with you….this time it's got to be goodbye.'*

Elton went on to write about his time in the hospital on its intensive and tough rehabilitation programme in his 2012 book, *'Love is the Cure: On Life, Loss and the End of AIDS'.*

In the book he says; *'My time at Parkside Lutheran was as challenging as it was transformative. The first days were especially difficult. When you deprive your body of cocaine after having used very much and very frequently, as I had, the craving for it is inconceivably enormous. I went through bouts of extreme anxiety and irritability. I couldn't sleep. I couldn't think about anything but my own misery.*

'This was compounded by the fact that I had stopped using not just cocaine but everything I had self-medicated with: the booze, the food, the sex. I was depressed and alone. I felt sick and weak and foggy. Needless to say, the first stages of rehab were among the most trying periods of my life.

'Every day of staying sober was a challenge, but it was invigorating to feel that I was regaining control over my life, my direction, my choices.'

After leaving hospital, clean at last, but still a work in progress, Elton returned to London.

He continued to work on his recovery and for years he attended supportive group meetings such as those organised by Alcoholics Anonymous.

By the end of 1990 Elton felt he was coming through and had been given a second chance. Not only had he shaken off his personal demons, but also he was relieved to have escaped an AIDS diagnosis.

He had been lucky and wanted to give something back. *'It's now my job to repay the debt'* he has said since.

While Elton was working on his recovery he obviously wasn't putting out much new music. Releases around that time include two compilation albums. The first, *'To Be Continued'* marked his 25 years in the business Secondly was *'The Very Best of Elton John'* which came out at Christmas 1990. This has gone on to be his best-selling album in the UK.

Two Rooms: Celebrating the Songs of Elton John & Bernie Taupin was released in 1991 as a tribute to the pair, as various artists covered their songs, including Kate Bush, The Who, Bon Jovi and Rod Stewart. The tribute was a touching recognition of their talent by fellow musical artists.

For his part Elton released The One in June 1992, including a collaboration with Eric Clapton, Runaway Train. The One spent three consecutive weeks at number two in the UK, and was his best-selling album in America since 1975, achieving twice platinum sales.

Through all the work, Elton remembered his pledge to put something back into society. In 1992 he set up the Elton John AIDS Foundation (EJAF) in the US and in the UK a year later. Based on the premise that AIDS can be beaten, EJAF says it acts on that belief by *'raising funds for evidence-based programs and policies and also by speaking out with honesty and compassion about the realities of people's lives.'*

And on his website Elton describes the EJAF as now being one of

← ———————————————————————— • • • •

Elton John attends the 1989 Victoires de la Musique ceremony

the *'largest, most respected and 'can-do' charities in its field'*.

Back to his day job, the Duets album was released in 1993 showcasing Elton's work with artists including k.d.laing and Gladys Knight and including the live version of *"Don't Let the Sun Go Down on Me"* with George Michael, which had already been number one in the UK and America. The album debuted at number seven in the UK.

Now rid of his demons and clean of substance abuse —he later described it as having, *'grown up at 43'* — Elton realised he was lonely. He was necessarily having to keep away from old habits and some of the friends who went with them, so on a whim one evening he phoned a friend in London and asked that they invite some new people over to him in Windsor for dinner.

Everything was organised accordingly and among the new faces Elton met during the evening was David Furnish, a Canadian advertising executive; an independent man with a career of his own. David was shy and rather quiet during the dinner, but Elton was immediately drawn to him and took his number. He called him as soon as was reasonable the next day and invited David to another dinner — this time for just the two of them.

The pair clicked immediately and after just a few months David moved in with Elton in Windsor. The pair have gone from strength to strength ever since and are now among the most influential couples in the world.

Elton's meeting with David triggered a new purple patch of success. Now settled and happy in his personal life, his debauchery behind him, Elton was better able to devote his still phenomenal energy to a new focus — writing for musical theatre.

This was a new challenge and professional direction for him, which began when Tim Rice, the celebrated lyricist most famous for his work with Andrew Lloyd Webber, phoned to ask if Elton would be interested in working with him on a new project for Disney — its animated film The Lion King.

Elton agreed — even though he was incredibly busy. Among other things he was preparing for a series of tours with fellow singer/songwriter/pianist Billy Joel. The pair went on to perform together on and off until 2010, and these *'Face to Face'* tours, became the longest running and most successful of their type in pop music history.

Elton had also embarked on his 25th studio album Made in England, which he dedicated to his new love David. The title track was the second single — a witty autobiographical song including the line *' I had a quit-me father and a love-me mother'*.

And he had been honoured with a place in the Rock and Roll Hall of Fame, having been inducted in 1994 during his first year of eligibility. During his acceptance speech Elton asked Bernie to join him on stage saying. *'I'm not very good with words. I have someone to write my words for me and without him the journey would not have been possible. Without Bernie there would not have been any Elton John at all. I love him dearly'*.

However, Elton's collaboration with Tim Rice was to prove incredibly successful too. His music combined with Tim's lyrics to produce one of the most successful soundtracks of all time, which triumphed at the 67th Academy Awards in 1995. Three of the five nominees for the Best Original Song Oscar were from the film's soundtrack. Elton and Tim won for Can You Feel The Love Tonight, beating their other tracks, Hakuna Matata and Circle of Life.

• • • ⟶

On stage, 1990

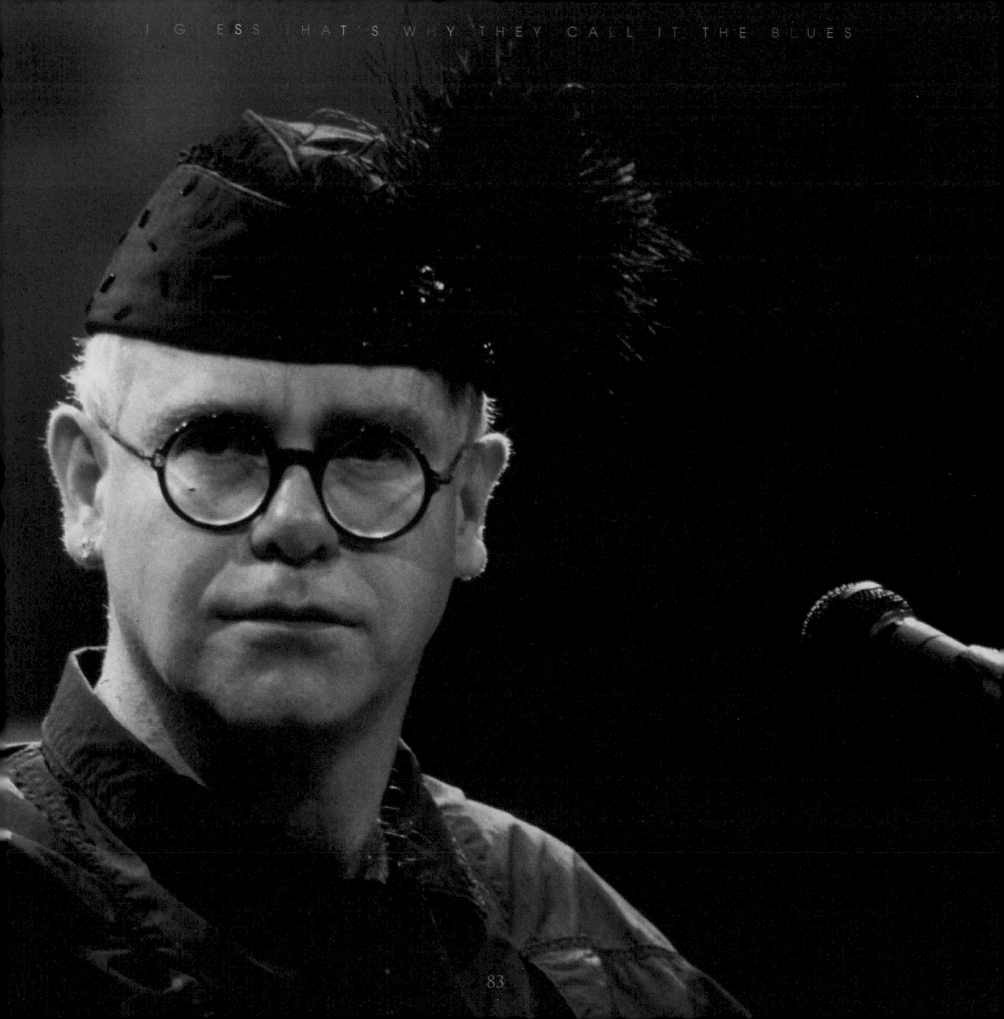

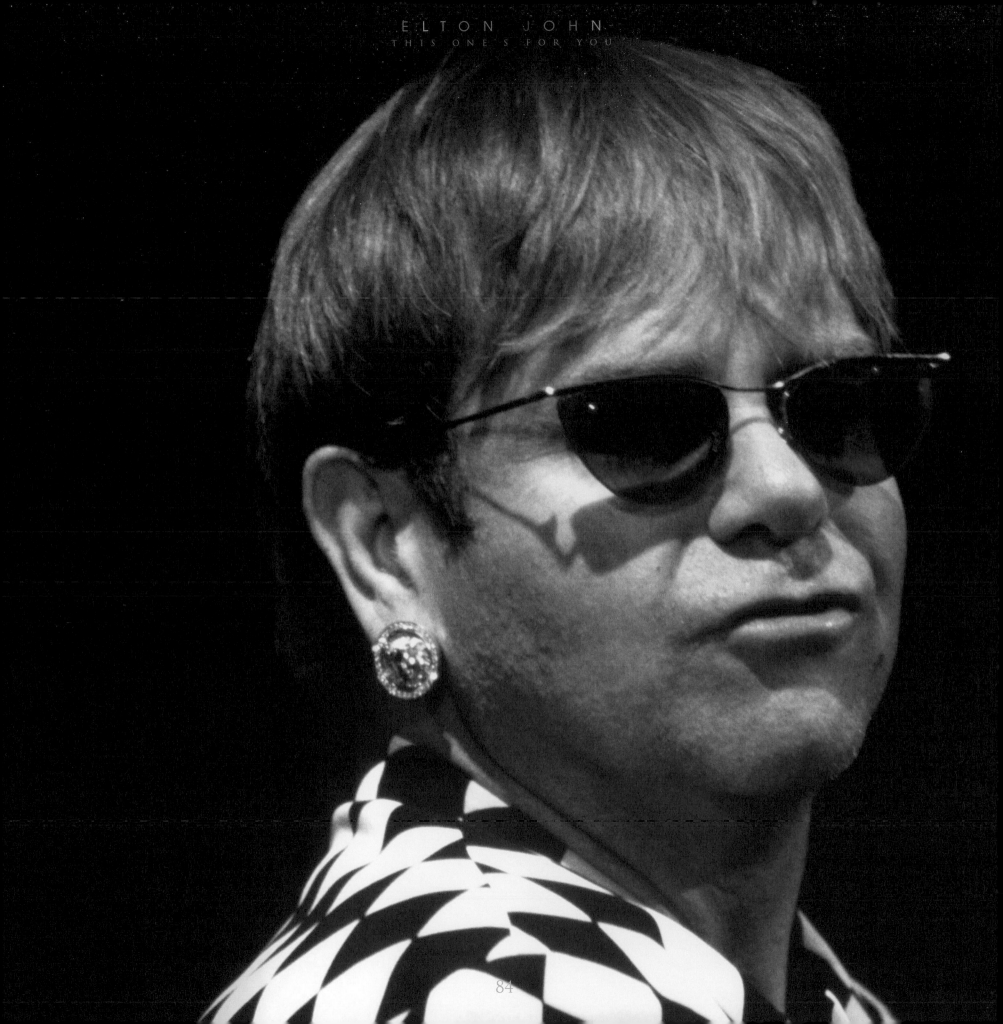

'This is such an exciting night,' an emotional Elton said during his acceptance speech, going on to thank his parents Sheila and Fred, David Furnish and John Reid in particular. He dedicated his award to his nan Ivy Sewell who had died the week before the ceremony.

Can you Feel the Love Tonight also won a Golden Globe award and gained the Best Male Pop Vocal prize at that year's Grammys. Together with Circle of Life it also became a hit single. The Lion King soundtrack went on to go diamond with sales of 15 million copies by 1999. Another award came from this work when, in 1996, The Walt Disney Company showed its appreciation for Elton's 'extraordinary and integral' contribution to its films and theatrical works by naming him a Disney Legend

Although now at a good place in his life, where drink and drugs no longer exacerbated his moods, Elton's mercurial nature remained and was perfectly captured in the famous 1996 documentary Tantrums and Tiaras made by David.

Having long harboured ambitions to be a film-maker David was the perfect choice to make the film showing a year in the life of Elton John. Elton said that he wanted the public to know more about him, rather than just his melodies, and trusted David to strike the right note.

With unprecedented 24/7 access to his subject, David came up with the goods, providing a fascinating, frank and funny portrait of Elton, warts and all.

The general public was already familiar with tabloid tales of his spending, said at one time to include £5,000 a week on fresh flowers and £250,000 shopping sprees with Gianni Versace. Elton is so rich that he must have stopped counting. Various estimates put his net worth at around £500 million.

But to see evidence of his wealthy lifestyle and possessions at first hand was truly revelatory.

Years later, discussing his spending in an interview with Piers Morgan in 2010 he answered his critics decisively saying; 'I have no guilt about it [spending money] I earn the money. I pay my taxes. I have never lived anywhere else but Britain. It goes back into the economy. What's the problem?'

Tantrums and Tiaras also showed him having two of his famed 'little moments'. The first shows him angrily pacing around while an assistant attempts to locate a missing bag 'I get up at 7 to do this and he leaves a bag in the car. I don't want to do it {making a video} any more' says Elton.

Later in the film he is shown in a fury during a holiday in the south of France, speechless with rage and only speaking again after calming down enough to order a plane home, saying 'I've had it with this place', after a woman had infuriated him by calling out while he was playing tennis.

But it also showed his kindness, his humour, his capacity to love and his incredible energy, passion for charity and dedication to his work.

Looking back at the film Elton acknowledges that some of his behaviour has been outrageous, but says that he also finds it funny.

Elton John performs at Shoreline Amphitheatre on September 15, 1995 in Mountain View California

FUNERAL FOR A FRIEND

1997 – 2007

Not so funny was 1997. Although it began in style, it ended in sadness as Elton lost two of his best friends, fashion designer Gianni Versace and Diana Princess of Wales within six weeks of each other.

Before both untimely deaths, Elton had celebrated his 50th birthday with a fabulous party in London. His prediction as a 26-year-old that in 25 years time he'd be back playing the piano in a pub somewhere had not come to pass and the occasion needed to be marked.

A star-studded celebration was arranged at the Hammersmith Palais where guests gathered for the arrival of the birthday boy.

It was worth the wait. Elton arrived in a giant truck which was entirely necessary to house his regal Louis XIV-style costume, comprising an outrageously high silver wig and an incredible 15ft long feather train attached to a stunning silver and pearl white brocade coat.

But just a few months later, in July, he was dressed in mourning at the funeral of his friend, the Italian fashion designer Gianni Versace, who had been assassinated aged 50 by an obsessed associate.

Elton was famously pictured with tears in his eyes, being comforted by Diana, Princess of Wales, another of their mutual friends.

He had known Princess Diana since they met in 1981 at Prince Andrew's 21st birthday party and it was friendship at first sight. The pair had lots in common, but unfortunately their shared traits included a tendency to freeze out people who upset them. They had fallen out over Versace's book Rock and Royalty — which was to benefit the Elton John AIDS Foundation — but were reconciled before Versace's funeral.

Barely six weeks later, Diana herself was killed in a car crash in Paris on August 31. The outpouring of public grief was unlike anything seen before and her funeral on September 6th was one of the biggest televised events in history, watched live by an estimated 2.5 billion people.

Elton was asked to perform at the service in Westminster Abbey and, wanting to pay tribute to his friend, thought that his 1973 hit Candle in the Wind would be a fitting piece. But it had to be reworked to be a more appropriate honour for a princess. So Bernie quickly rewrote the lyrics, including the new opening line; *'Goodbye England's rose'*, may you ever grow in our hearts. The title was changed to Candle in the Wind 1997.

As well as the billions watching in other countries, an estimated one million people lined the streets of London — many openly weeping — and another 32 million of Elton's countrymen and women were watching at home. The atmosphere in the Abbey, packed with two thousand mourners — including of course her two young sons — was equally emotional.

It was one of the hardest performances of his life. But Elton knew he had to hold it together and he sang out strongly; his voice only cracking, just slightly, once.

The song proved to be the perfect epitaph and Elton the perfect choice to sing it. His iconic and moving performance completed his redemption among the British general public. He was singing for them — and became a national treasure.

Asked later how he stayed calm during the performance, he put it down to his professional experience. *'I knew that I couldn't afford to be emotional,'* he said. *'I wasn't singing it for myself, I was representing my country. I had to deliver.'*

But as a consummate professional he was aware of the pitfalls and for the first time in his life requested a teleprompter, purely to ensure that he didn't revert to the original *'Marilyn lyrics'* out of habit.

After the funeral Elton went to the Townhouse Studies in West London and recorded the new version as a single which has gone on to sell an astounding 33 million copies. This makes it the biggest-selling single in the world since UK and US singles charts began in the 1950s.

All royalties, which now top £100 million, go to the Diana, Princess of Wales Memorial Fund.

Elton has never sung the 1997 version since, preferring to use the original at concerts.

Elton also lost another old friend and former confidante in the nineties — although this time by design. To the amazement of the music industry in May 1998, he announced that he was parting company with John Reid, his manager of almost three decades.

Initially the split was described as amicable, but afterwards there was a more public fall out and a court case over a financial dispute.

Happier events of 1997 were to follow. Chief among them was the opening of The Lion King musical on Broadway and the release of Elton's 25th album, The Big Picture, which enjoyed some commercial success and included Something About The Way You Look Tonight which was the other track on the double A-side Candle In The Wind 1997 single.

Elton went on tour in North America and Europe to promote the album, as well as performing more Face to Face concerts with Billy Joel.

Another happier brush with royalty came in February 1998 when Elton was knighted for his services to music and charity. After the ceremony at Buckingham Palace, to which Elton took David and his mother Sheila and stepfather Fred, Elton said; *'I love my country and to be recognised in such a way — I can't think of anything better.'*

He kept working at a pace and never let up on his fundraising efforts, performing concerts and selling more of his possessions for charity.

However he did have to take a break after suffering a health scare in the summer of 1999. On his way to perform at the wedding of Spice Girl Victoria Adams to David Beckham, Elton was taken ill and tests revealed he was suffering from an irregular heartbeat.

The fitting of a pacemaker successfully righted the problem and he returned to work with vigour.

He was well again in good time for the opening of The Lion King in London's West End in 1999 and then to continue his new adventures in musical theatre by contributing songs to the DreamWorks animation The Road to Eldorado.

He collaborated with Tim Rice again and composed the music for a Disney version of Aida. The score and the cast-recording went on to win a Tony and a Grammy award respectively and the show opened on Broadway in March 2000.

That same year Elton released Elton John One Night Only — The Greatest Hits Live — which was recorded on 20 and 21 October 2000 at his beloved venue Madison Square Garden in New York.

Working well with Bernie again, Elton released his 26th studio album Songs from the West Coast, in October 2001. This marked a return to a slightly stripped-down, more piano-heavy sound and gained critical acclaim as being one of the strongest of his career. The stand out track I Want Love was a hit in 2001, with the accompanying video also making an impact as it was directed by British film artist Sam Taylor-Wood and featured the actor Robert Downey Jnr, recently out of rehab himself, wandering through an empty mansion lip- synching the vocal.

Building on this resurgence, a fifth UK number one single came in 2003 when a re-released version of Are You Ready For Love topped the charts. Elton had first recorded the song in 1977 during the Thom Bell sessions in Philadelphia. But when it was first released in 1979 it had failed to trouble the charts.

But in 2003 Sky Sports chose the single for an advert to promote its coverage of the forthcoming football season, using the tagline, *'We're ready, are you?'* thus giving the number a new lease of life.

Elton maintained an incredible schedule of live shows, also fitting in 75 performances of The Red Piano show in 2004, 2005 and 2006 in Las Vegas . He released his 27th studio album in 2004, Peachtree Road, which only reached 21 in the UK album charts and received lukewarm reviews. Yet, as Elton sings on the opening track Weight Of The World, *'Fortune and fame are so fleeting these days, I'm happy to say I'm amazed that I'm still around'*, going on to sing that he was *'Happy today, happy to play, With the weight of the world off of my back'*.

He dedicated this album to his old friend and producer Gus Dudgeon who aged just 59 had been killed in a car crash along with his wife Sheila in July 2002.

The album fared better in America than it had in the UK, reaching number 17.

Amid several autobiographic and reflective elements to this album, Bernie gives Elton an apposite lyric in celebration of his life with David, in My Elusive Drug, where he describes swapping his habits for his new found love.

While never easing up on his frenetic schedule of touring and recording, Elton found time to notch up another musical theatre triumph in 2005.

This time working with lyricist Lee Hall, Elton co-wrote the music for the international smash hit stage production of Billy Elliot the Musical.

The score gave him another top five hit in the UK with his version of the number Electricity.

The tale of a talented young working class boy desperate to become a ballet dancer against the wishes of his dismayed coalminer father had resonance for Elton and he sang the song with real feeling.

The show won the 2006 Laurence Olivier Award, for Best New Musical and went to run in the West End for 11 years. It has gone on to open all over the world including a four-year run on Broadway. Another musical, Lestat —a collaboration on a show based on the book The Vampire Chronicles, written with Bernie — had a brief run on Broadway in 2006.

Yet all the success and accolades Elton was enjoying from this new stream of musical theatre work were to pale in comparison to the happiness he felt at the end of 2005.

Following a change to the law to allow legal partnerships for same sex couples, Elton and David, formed a civil partnership at the very first opportunity on December 21, 2005. It was a happy day, both men wore dark suits, the only hint of a colourful adornment being Elton's purple shaded glasses and a glitzy brooch on his jacket.

Just seven people made the guest list for the ceremony in Windsor at the Guildhall — Elton's mother Sheila, and stepfather Fred; David's parents Jack and Gladys; the artist Sam Taylor-Wood and

her husband Jay Joplin; publisher Sandy Brant, along with the couple's spaniel Arthur.

Music remained central to his life and in 2006 Elton released The Captain & the Kid— the second autobiographical album with Bernie — which was a thoughtful examination of their careers since Captain Fantastic and the Brown Dirt Cowboy back in 1975. It reached number six in the UK, and number 18 in the US.

In 2007 a contented Elton celebrated his 60th birthday by playing his 60th concert at New York's Madison Square Garden his self-declared 'favourite venue in the whole wide world'.

• • • • •

• • • • ⟶

Sir Elton John arrives at the opening of Sir Elton John and Amnesty International's Human Rights Action Centre, celebrating the opening of the new building in Shoreditch on May 18, 2005 in London

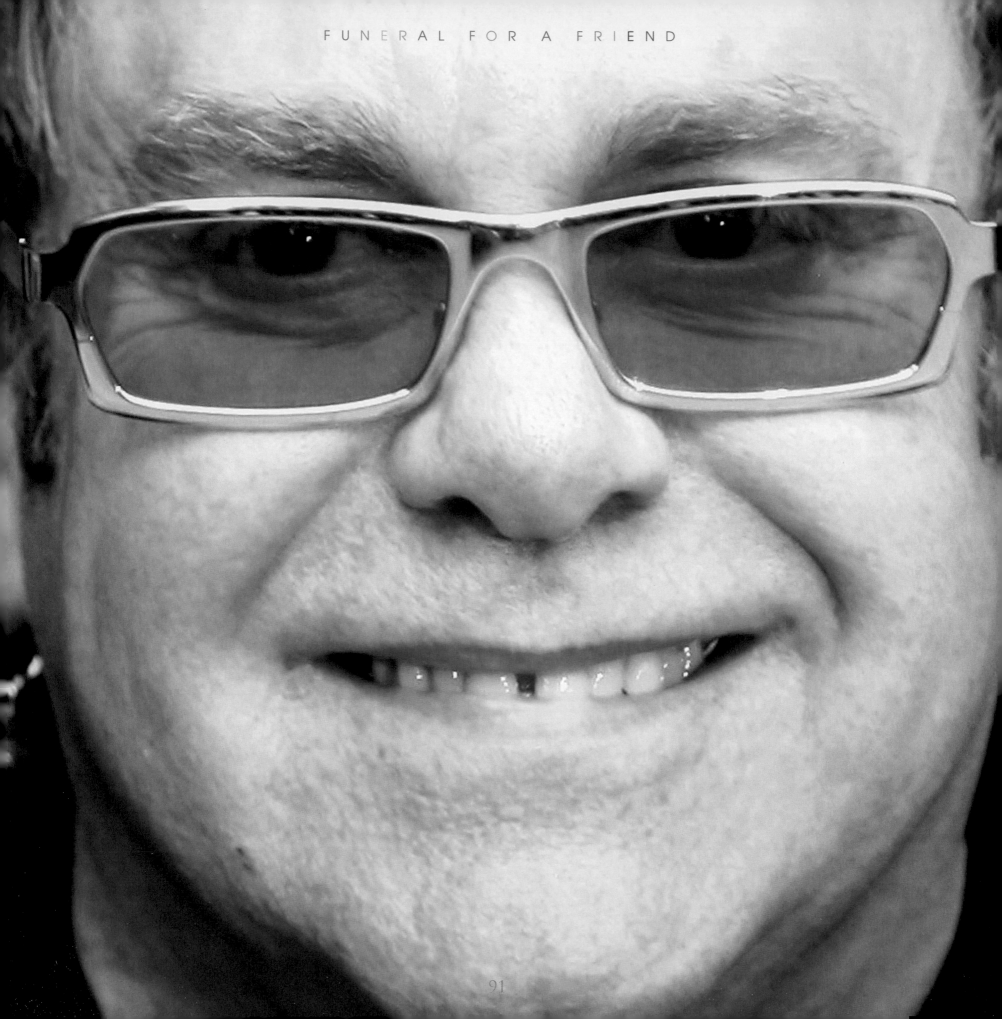

BLESSED

n the 10 years he had so far spent with David, Elton had settled down and credits his husband with truly changing his life for the better.

While acquainting David with his musical history and influences, Elton was inspired to get in touch with Leon Russell who had been such a hero to him when he was young. The two made an album of soulful duets together, The Union which was positively reviewed, entered the American charts at number three, and also made Rolling Stone magazine's list of the 30 Best Albums of that year.

Just when you would think that Elton must have ticked off everything on his bucket list, he came up with another surprise. He and David welcomed the arrival of a son, Zachary Jackson Levon born through a surrogate, on Christmas Day 2010.

His brother, Elijah Joseph Daniel, followed three years later on January 11, 2013.

Speaking to The Mirror newspaper, Elton explained how the children had changed his outlook: "I've learned that the simplest things in life, like having a minute with them, are worth more than any painting, any photograph, any house or hit record. Before we had the children we just had our lives and we would spend money because we didn't have anything else to focus on.

'We have really toned things down because we have enough stuff. There is nothing else we need.'

He was still on cloud nine about his life two years later when speaking on the Ellen DeGeneres Show in America he said; 'If you had said to me 10 years ago I'd be sitting on your show married to the man I love and have two beautiful children I would have said,

'You put acid in my drink'. But life throws you challenges and life throws you curveballs – and great curveballs'.

'These two children have come along at a time I never thought I'd have children. They are the greatest thing in our lives. There's no words to describe how much we love these boys — they are just amazing'.

When asked if his children were musical Elton said he wouldn't push them in any direction whatsoever. 'They sing Rocket Man, Don't Go Breaking My Heart and Bennie and the Jets. They love music but they are not that interested in what I do. They are kind of more interested in their Lego, which is fine with me,' he said.

With everything in his life changing, and loving his new role and responsibilities as a father, Elton took a break from recording.

But he did make time to work on the successful Rocket Pictures soundtrack for the animated movie Gnomeo and Juliet, and to perform to an audience of millions at a concert to mark Queen Elizabeth II Diamond Jubilee at Buckingham Palace on June 4, 2012.

Ever eager to remain current, Elton also produced an album with Pnau — a dance duo he had been mentoring for several years. It is a remix of various Elton songs from his early years which made its debut at number one on the UK charts. AllMusic described it as being 'inventive and fun' while NME said it 'subverts Elton's reputation as a cosy British institution'.

Elton's appetite for new music is still voracious. Every week he listens to the new music that's been issued — preferring a CD to a digital track.

Elton & Lady Gaga perform during the 52nd Annual
Grammy Awards, January 31, 2010 in Los Angeles

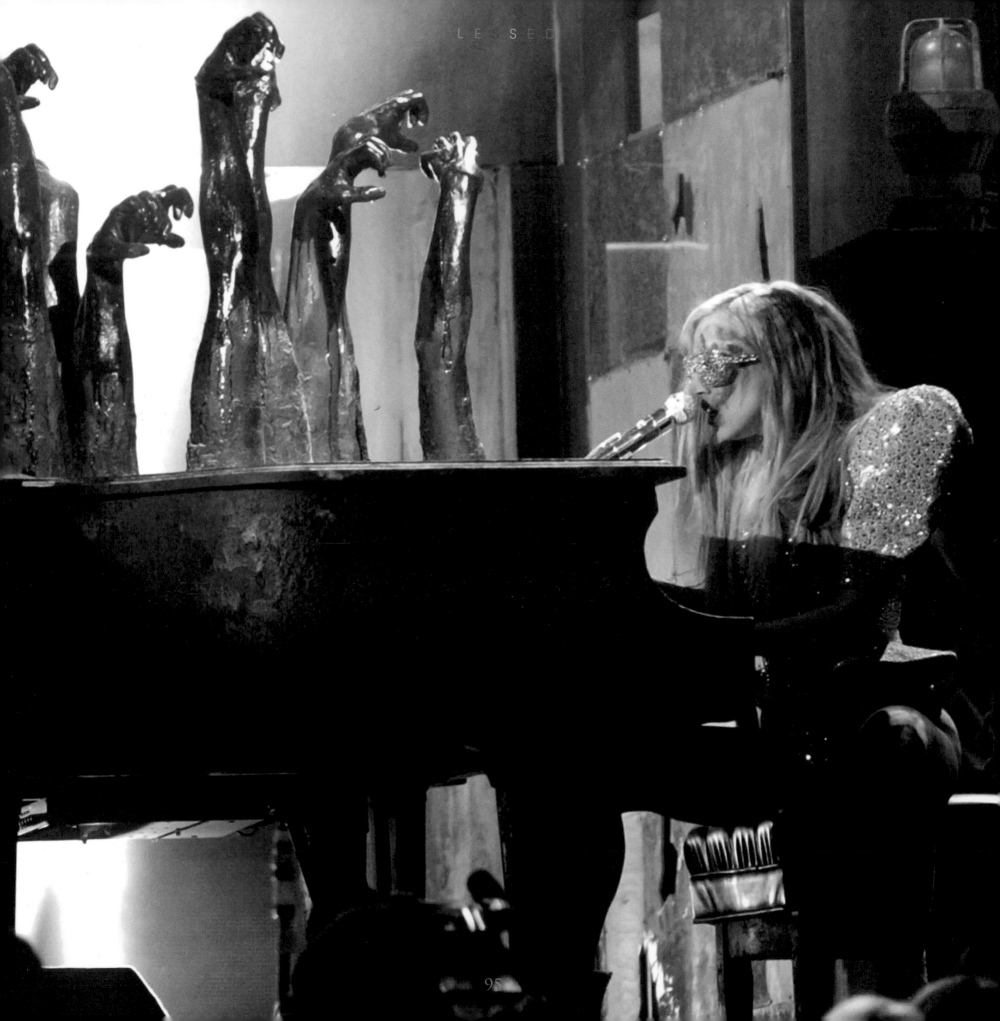

He went back into the studio himself the following year to record his 29th studio album The Diving Board. The Ultimate Classic Rock review described it as *'simply a fine set of new music from a pair of brilliant songwriters'*. Again its lyrics from Bernie contained some slightly dark reflections and observations on lives well lived, and Elton's melodies were popularly piano-driven.

Outside of music, Elton was delighted when in 2014 Watford Football Club named a stand after him. Despite having given up his club chairmanship in 2002 because of time pressures, Elton still loved the team and is Honorary Life-President. He described the day of the stand's dedication, which he attended with David and his sons, as being one of the greatest of his life. *'Watford Football Club is forever in my heart'* Elton told the crowd.

Another health scare caused him to pause in April 2017 when he fell ill on a return flight from Chile after a South American tour. It turned out he had contracted a rare and potentially deadly bacterial infection, necessitating two nights in intensive care and the subsequent cancellation of all his concerts for the next two months. Happily he made a complete recovery.

But then there was more upset for Elton at the end of the year when his mother Sheila died aged 92 on December 4.

Elton notified his fans with a tweet which read: *'So sad to say that my mother passed away this morning. I only saw her last Monday and I am in shock. Travel safe Mum. Thank you for everything. I will miss you so much. Love, Elton.'*

There had been a period of froideur between the pair for several years, following a disagreement after Sheila refused Elton's request

to cut her ties with two former members of his circle, his former driver-turned PA Bob Halley and old manager John Reid.

But even throughout their estrangement Elton continued to support her financially and the pair were reconciled before Mothers Day in America in May 2017 when Elton messaged her publicly through social media, saying ; *'Dear mum Happy Mother's Day! So happy we are back in touch. Love, Elton'*

After her funeral on 3 January 2018 Elton wrote on Instagram: *'Dear Mum, Today's funeral was perfect. Having the service in the family chapel and attended by your brother and sister brought us all comfort. Having the service where Nan lived out her final days brought you and your Mother back together again. Tomorrow your friends will gather separately to say their goodbyes. I've chosen all the music so everything will be just right.'* He concluded: *'Thank you for bringing me into the world and for all that you have done for me. Love, Elton #RIP'*

There had been no such tributes to his father Stanley, who had died of heart disease back in 1991. Elton did not go to see him during his illness, nor did he attend the funeral, although he did send a message to Edna and her four sons.

Back in the recording studio in 2018 he produced his 33rd album Wonderful Crazy Night. Reflecting Elton's new happiness with life, it was a happy up-tempo record, sounding like more traditional rock and roll and received generally favourable reviews

'I think it sounds more like a 70's record made in 2018,' said Elton.

Evidently his great fervour to make music was undiminished. So his next move took fans by surprise.

Elton John performs at PPL Center on September 27, 2016 in Allentown, Pennsylvania

FAREWELL

YELLOW

BRICK

ROAD

'It was *a pretty easy decision to be honest* with you'

So said Elton on 24 January 2018 as he announced he was to bow out of performing live to spend more time with his children.

But after nearly 50 years on the road and some 3,500 concerts, Elton could not leave the stage without one last hurrah. He planned to say his goodbyes to fans via the massive 'Farewell Yellow Brick Road' tour consisting of more than 300 shows over three years across five continents; North America, Europe and the Middle East, Asia, South America and Australasia.

The concerts kicked off in September 2018 and continue until 2021, promising to take fans on 'a musical and highly visual journey spanning a 50-year career of hits like no one has ever seen before'.

Reviewing the opening night of the tour in Pennsylvania USA, Rolling Stone magazine said the show was; 'the most bombastic, elaborate, high-tech arena show he's ever attempted'.

A farewell involving Elton was never going to be anything other than a huge spectacular.

The production is extravagant, including a platform to move his gold-framed piano from one side of the stage to the other and a massive video screen displaying videos and specially commissioned films. At one point the screen appears to reflect Elton playing live at the piano, the difference being that the piano on the screen is on fire, while fortunately the one on the stage is not.

But despite all the tricks and theatrics the main focus is, of course, the music.

His band includes old retainers Davey Johnstone, Nigel Olsson and Ray Cooper.

Although himself famously not in the business of looking back, Elton acknowledges that the fans want to hear their most favourite songs and has weighted the set list heavily towards his 1970's heyday — even the most recent hit he plays, *'Believe'*, dates from 1995's Made In England album.

After performing his final numbers dressed in a kimono, Elton disrobes and is left wearing a tracksuit with his name emblazoned across the back. He then mounts a gold platform that carries him off into a hole in the screen, in the manner of the disappearing Wizard of Oz of Yellow Brick Road fame.

NME described the farewell concert as *'stunning and satisfying'*.

It is a fitting farewell for an artist ranked by Billboard magazine in the US as the most successful male solo artist on its list of Hot 100 Greatest All-time Artists and third overall, behind the Beatles and Madonna.

He is also an inductee into the Songwriters Hall of Fame and is a Fellow of the British Academy of Songwriters, Composers and Authors.

Despite this incredible level of worldwide acclaim, combined with wealth and superstar status, Elton still sees himself as a singer/songwriter at heart and remains a massive music fan. He still gets a thrill from hearing new music and many a nascent artist has received a surprise call of encouragement from him.

His bond with Bernie is as strong as ever. In a tribute to his